© Manuela Böhme

Kankyo Tannier is a Buddhist nun of the Zen tradition. She lived for over fifteen years in a monastery in the French region of Alsace before moving to the heart of a nearby forest, where she lives in a little house in close contact with the trees and animals. She teaches meditation courses and writes a blog on everyday spirituality at www.dailyzen.fr.

The Gift
of
Silence

Kankyo Tannier

The Gift
of
Silence

Finding Peace in a World full of Noise

Translated by Alan Thawley

yellow
kite

First published in Great Britain in 2018 by Yellow Kite
An imprint of Hodder & Stoughton
An Hachette UK company

1

2017, © Editions First, an imprint of Edi8, Paris, France

Translation copyright © Alan Thawley 2017

The right of Kankyo Tannier to be identified as the
Author of the Work has been asserted by her in accordance
with the Copyright, Designs and Patents Act 1988.

A CIP catalogue record for this title is available from the British Library

ISBN 978 1 473 67343 4
eBook ISBN 978 1 473 67346 5

Typeset in Optima by
Palimpsest Book Production Ltd, Falkirk, Stirlingshire

Printed and bound in Great Britain by Clays Ltd, St Ives plc

Hodder & Stoughton policy is to use papers that are natural, renewable
and recyclable products and made from wood grown in sustainable
forests. The logging and manufacturing processes are expected to
conform to the environmental regulations of the country of origin.

Yellow Kite
Hodder & Stoughton Ltd
Carmelite House
50 Victoria Embankment
London EC4Y 0DZ

www.yellowkitebooks.co.uk

My dear disciples, over crowds, choose solitude.
Over agitation, choose calm
Over clamour, choose silence.

The last words of the Buddha, quoted by Zen master
Olivier Reigen Wang-Genh whilst teaching.

Contents

Introduction

A DIFFERENT KIND OF BOOK

Personal development books are often full of steps to follow that supposedly bring us serenity in the space of a few days. Besides the fact that it took the Buddha himself – something of an expert in his field – several years, I wasn't convinced that such manuals, with their 'ready-made' solutions, were up to the task. I thought a different kind of book was needed.

The theme of silence seemed to appear to me all by itself, as if there was a benevolent deity answering to the cry of despair from a desperate nun who could no longer stand the cacophony around her. Whichever way I looked, I saw a lack of calm and well-being in modern society, a world where our relentless activities have turned the volume right up to unbearable levels. With people increasingly plugged into their devices, headphones on to create a reassuring sonic cocoon, silence seemed to have been consigned to oblivion. So I wondered, how would it be if we all relearnt the art of silence, making it the defining practice of the 21st century? A new way of being, perhaps – a revolution!

The approach that I have followed over the years, and that I am sharing with you in this book, has taught me to embrace silence and discover the immense power we all have hidden within ourselves. Through nothing more than heartfelt effort and repetition, you can choose to walk this same path, and I can reassure you that just behind the next hill is a stunning view . . .

Imagine I am giving you the keys to a building – it is large and there are many doors, but you can choose to open some and leave others closed; it's up to you. And later you can come back and explore some more, because by the end of the book you will have a whole bunch of keys at your disposal.

In my own reading I have often had to suppress the desire to respond with a resounding 'Prove it!' to all those zealous champions of a certain 'miracle method', whose lives all too rarely reflect this supposed wisdom, so I have alternated anecdotes drawn from real life with some little exercises. To avoid the wrath of the more sceptical amongst you, I have included plenty of examples and first-hand accounts . . . and without leaving out the failures, however ignominious!

Here and there, this book also contains a few flights of lyricism, outpourings spontaneously inspired by my sense of wonder in the presence of nature or the beauty of my fellow beings. For the more rational souls amongst you, I leave it entirely up to you to skip merrily past these offending passages like mountain goats: the author will not hold it against you (and indeed will know nothing about it!).

As you read through these pages – methodically or otherwise – you will find a number of practical exercises. Beware! Each one of these offers nothing less than the power to change your life! Because if I was going to write a book, devoting long sections to the benefits of certain practices and revealing large chunks of my personal life, I decided it might as well be worth the effort. So you open this book at your own peril. Profound changes lie in wait. A common theory in therapy is that many people prefer a disagreeable but familiar situation to something new but unpredictable. Does that sound like you?

Whilst a part of your brain is carefully considering that question, let me tell you a little about these exercises. They have been designed to be easy to integrate into your day. No need to get up before dawn or free up hours of your schedule in order to include my suggested practices in your daily routine. Think more in terms of sprinkling little touches of awareness and concentration into your normal activities, like a subtle spice added to a dish. Try it and see: it can bring a new taste to your day, revealing some surprising flavours.

Sometimes, of course, taking more time to do things, savouring periods of luxurious emptiness, can be even more beneficial. For those fortunate enough to have a little free time (count yourselves lucky in our hyperactive society!) we will talk about monastic or silent retreats in the home, lasting just one or several days.

I hope that each of you will find in the following pages some ideas or exercises that suit you. Think of them as little nuggets you carry secretly in your pocket – a way of touching base with your rich inner world.

AN APOLOGY FROM THE AUTHOR

A book about silence containing over 30,000 words. Quite a paradox, isn't it? All these pages to describe the inexpressible when a Rembrandt painting or an Erik Satie piano piece would have said it all. And in fact, nothing could be simpler than inviting silence to life's feast: a fraction of a second of attention, ears that wake up and start to listen, a bird flying across the sky . . . or anything else that is spontaneous enough to take us by surprise.

But when it comes to painting or pirouetting my fingers across a piano keyboard, I have all the delicacy of a scrum half in the French rugby XV and the calm of a football coach on the touchline. So I have had to make do with the means at my disposal: words that emerge exuberantly as if by magic, skipping merrily right to left, up and down, back and forth, until they find their place on the page. Ideas, phrases and anecdotes have poured out one after the other, gradually stitching together the fabric of this book. I have been quite amazed to witness all this, asking myself this underlying question: where do all these words come from? What is this consciousness responsible for these words, this writing, this chatter? The mystery remains unsolved, but the result is the book you are holding in your hands, and whose tendency towards verbosity you will, I hope, excuse.

MY FIRST STEPS ALONG THE ZEN PATH

But this story begins much longer ago . . .

I was raised in a Catholic family in the suburbs of Paris: an environment imbued with a brand of working-class Catholicism more interested in trade unionism than bible study. I learnt a lot from my upbringing, including what would later become the bedrock of my spirituality: mutual assistance, fraternity, living in harmony and . . . prayer. So the first wafts of incense I breathed in every Sunday at mass as a baby in my father's arms probably contributed to my future monastic career just as much as the Buddhist writings I immersed myself in during my studies. Back then, ours was a richly vibrant, convivial parish, and I remember street parties with representatives of every continent and every skin colour.

In my teenage years, however, I parted ways with Catholicism. I wasn't satisfied with the answers I received on issues such as social justice, life after death, or even the more general 'meaning of life'. But above all, I wanted to explore different continents. And Buddhism – which I came across in the Dalai Lama's books – seemed to me to be a suitably distant land for a fresh start. This was the beginning of my adventure – I threw myself into Asian spirituality with undisguised enthusiasm.

After graduating in public law, I dutifully started work as a journalist and singing teacher. But in parallel, I very soon found myself drawn towards Zen monasteries, attending retreats in different parts of France. The desire for spirituality was too intense for me to carry on leading an 'ordinary' life. Day after day, I felt as if I was guided by a force inside, inviting me – with a sly little grin – to change my life. So after five or six of these Buddhist retreats, my wandering came to an end in Alsace, at the Ryumonji Zen monastery, where Master Olivier Reigen Wang-Genh welcomed me warmly, and I discovered a motivated and dynamic team.

And there I stayed for sixteen years: sixteen years of intense monastic life and mind-blowing apprenticeship. I'll tell you all about it in another book. But right now, let's get back to silence . . .

THE VARIOUS HATS I WEAR IN LIFE

When people ask me what I do, I always want to reply: 'Well, all kinds of things. I walk, I eat, I sleep, I look at the sky, I breathe, I stroke my cats, I meditate, I sing . . . What about you?' But that isn't what they want to hear. When talking to other people, everyone has to decide which hat they are wearing, so that they can be put into a nice little pigeonhole. I always think of it more as sticking a label to my forehead, and it seems we find people without a label disturbing. So to reassure those around me, I have adopted my own sticky labels that can be taken off and repositioned according to circumstances.

Most often, I wear the label that reads 'Zen Buddhist nun'. It's probably the one that has penetrated the deepest, ultimately coming to resemble more of a permanent tattoo than a temporary transfer. For the past fifteen years, this has been my noble occupation, although the word 'nun' is not entirely appropriate. Whilst it nicely captures the profoundly spiritual aspect of my life, it overlooks several things. In my Zen tradition, as in other Buddhist schools, we are allowed to marry (I have an extremely charming partner) and have children (I have chosen not to), whilst a great many of us carry on a professional activity outside of our monastic roles. So the word nun starts to sound a little behind the times, all the more so when you discover that I spend part of my time working on the internet. Besides my blog, I look after the social networks for the monastery and other Buddhist associations. A nun for the 21st century, if you like, with one foot in the ancient world and one very much in the modern one (which presents me with a very pleasing day-to-day challenge and calls for a good sense of balance!).

Other activities have also developed over the years and occupy more and more of my time: welcoming new people to the monastery, teaching meditation, giving talks, holding interviews, writing magazine articles, discussing with colleagues, etc. As a result, my days are busy and very, very interesting!

Sometimes, I wear the therapy label on my forehead. For several years, I have worked as a hypnotherapist, a branch of behavioural therapy that uses altered states of consciousness to bring about changes. It is used in a huge variety of areas: for depression, studying for exams, self-confidence, the treatment of phobias . . . The work fascinates me, and the knowledge I gain about people provides me with a wealth of material to feed into my Buddhist teachings. In the Zen tradition I follow, we work for a living for a few hours a week, because our spirituality is too recent for monks and nuns to receive financial support from a religious organisation in the way that the more traditional clergy do. And all the better for it! The fact that we have to experience the same difficulties as our fellow citizens around us – finding a job and earning some money – means that we are perhaps more in touch with everyday concerns in our discussions, talks and other teachings.

At other times, I teach singing and public speaking, which was how I began my career back in 1998 – a subject I will return to later in the book.

Finally, for the past two years, I have worked as a volunteer – looking after horses. A far cry from my other labels! Getting to know horses living semi-wild in their natural element has been such a learning experience that I won't deny myself the pleasure of telling you about it at length. And yet, like a good city girl, my knowledge of the world of horses had previously been limited to 'My Little Pony' toys and betting shop posters . . . These days, I'm regularly to be found with my backside on a tractor seat, taking hay to the fields, or with my fingers in a horse's mouth, checking the state of its teeth. I brush their coats, concoct 'digestion and well-being' mixtures to help them get through the winter, stroke them, scratch their itches, tickle them to their hearts' content and, above all, spend hours in their company, studying . . . what else but silence?

And now, here I am, a writer. If Victor Hugo will forgive such a bold claim! We should perhaps just move on . . .

THE WRITING COMMITTEE

Numerous people and certain other contributors have played their part in writing this book. Lala, my feline princess, for example, who inspired me to take breaks by regularly stretching out lazily by my computer. Without her and her kindly suggestions, my back would be in shreds . . . Her elegant pacing from one side of the office to the other also provided me with yoga exercises for the eyes, allowing me to rest my pupils.

Then there was the 93-year-old lady I met in the local tea room, who proclaimed in her magnificent Alsatian accent, 'I read what you write in the evenings, before I go to sleep, with a magnifying glass. It does me good . . . Oh, yes . . . No doubt about it: it does me good.' She restored my motivation when I started to flag.

There's the winter sun shining through the window pane on a grey day and falling on to my desk, as if to say, 'Come on, let's go! Time for work!'

There's the invisible bond with Sophie R., my first reader, who's often in my thoughts.

There are my friends, the wind, the birds, cafés, horses, social networks and, above all, the shelves full of books I've devoured since the age of five, when my wonderful granny taught me to read, comfortably ensconced on her lap. Without all those books, without those words that disappeared into the abysses of my little head, without these expressions that have happily emerged from the depths of my memory to be set down on these pages, the pages in question would have remained blank. And perhaps silent?

Then there are the residents of the monastery who patiently watched me go from one place to another, from the forest to the refectory, from the horses to the dojo, a pen in my hand and my head full of ideas. For a while, I haven't had much time for day-to-day practice, but have observed their commitment to the community from a distance, full of gratitude.

And then there is you, my soulmate and companion at my side all these years, and about whom I will say nothing. My silence envelops you, *I Shin Den Shin**, and this book is dedicated to you.

SOME OF MY PREFERRED PLACES TO WRITE

In order to produce this little spiritual manifesto, I have lugged my laptop to all kinds of places, in town and country.

To the Weiterswiller Zen monastery, for example, where I lived for over fifteen years. It's a magical place in Alsace, in the Northern Vosges mountains, hidden away on the edge

....

* I Shin Den Shin: a famous Zen expression referring to silent communication, from one heart to another.

of a forest. I'm still a very frequent visitor, particularly in the winter, when my little cottage turns into an icebox. Last winter, with temperatures regularly dipping down towards -10°C, frozen pipes and an icy wind blowing through the wooden walls, I gave up on my hermit's life to take refuge in the monastery and watch, safe and warm, as the wintry weather passed on by. In this environment, time has a very special quality. We're connected to the world and current events thanks to the internet, but the monastery itself exudes a peaceful energy that invites us to slow down. The place is imbued with good, positive vibrations which, when combined with meditation morning and evening, allows the mind to find some calm at long last.

And once a week, I would go to Strasbourg to write in the city's watering holes: *Le Michel* (the famous brasserie frequented by student protesters back in the May '68 uprising), *La Solidarité*, with its vast windows, and *L'Atlantico* (a bar on a barge with views over the river), as well as the Zen Buddhist Centre, our meditation space in the heart of the city. Stringing together sentences in a café, surrounded by students, cycle couriers and office workers, to a soundtrack of reggae or R&B, can be a real kick! Whilst the world rushes around, and time whizzes past faster than ever, in a little corner of the bar, a merry revolutionary (yours truly) discreetly settles into another space-time. She eats her lunch slowly, carefully observes the people around her, savours the atmosphere of the moment and – most importantly – takes her time. Allows herself the time to write, the time to listen to the space between two sentences, the time to smile at passers-by and the time to realise that noise can in fact be the best showcase for silence. The noisier the city, the more your inner silence reveals itself, in perfect symmetry.

But nothing is simple in this earthly life, and the 'rural' sections were sometimes written in town and vice versa . . .

HOW TO USE THIS BOOK

Most of the subjects and exercises described in this book are illustrated with examples taken from real life. This is based on a simple principle: if someone has successfully tested something, the door is wide open for others to walk through. When I was studying hypnosis, we thoroughly explored the field of neuro-linguistic programming (NLP), which is a bit of a mouthful but simply refers to a sort of brain training. So I learnt how our cranium works, aside from the purely medical aspects and, most importantly, the correct way to direct it towards the goals we want to achieve. It's amazingly effective! One of the principles of NLP is 'modelling'. To achieve a goal, make progress in a given area or make changes to our lives, the creators of NLP simply suggest looking at people who have successfully achieved these goals . . . and imitating them! They dressed it up by calling the technique modelling, but we're really only talking about learning by imitation. In French society, where revolutionary spirit and independent thinking are worn as something of a badge of honour, the idea of having a model or imitating someone doesn't always go down too well, as if it were only for the weak-minded. 'No god, no master', by all means, but we still need something to admire.

So after my studies, I started modelling others with a vengeance. The minute someone did something interesting or showed a particular talent, I carefully studied their behaviour to capture the substance of their approach. Some of the people I spoke to must have grown sick of my questions. Take a certain nun by the name of Michèle, who would remain completely unflappable in the face of unkind remarks made by one of her colleagues. I invited her out for a cup of tea and grilled her about it at length. 'How do you manage not to get annoyed?', 'What do you feel on an emotional level?', 'What do you think about yourself, or about that woman, when she's nasty to you?', 'How do you put it out of your mind?', etc. She showed great patience throughout this barrage of unexpected questions, and I was able to learn a huge amount by imitating her behaviour.

That's what I suggest you do with this book. When you find an example that speaks to you, imitate it! Model it, explore it, join the adventure! In doing so, you'll discover new resources, new ways of seeing the world, that you, in turn, will be able to adapt and, most importantly, share.

PART ONE

What is silence?

$$\left(1\right)$$

The virtue of silence

I t's 6pm in my little Alsace village. Night is falling, plunging the forest into a mellow twilight. A gentle breeze in the trees, the ringing of the bells of the Catholic church in the distance, followed by the echo from the bells of the Protestant church. The birds have fallen silent. A few rustles and the odd snapping sound betray the presence of wild animals. Around here, you often come across deer or wild boar, not to mention impressive numbers of birds of prey, crows and wandering cats. Dusk is calm, as if time were in suspense: winter is such a restful time for those able to hear it!

Because this is what we'll be talking about: relearning how to hear. To hear the silence, the space between words, the calm in the storm, and the passage of time. Relearning to appreciate things: the flavour of a moment, the aroma of a meal, the drift of the day and the warmth of the fire. Relearning how to feel: the touch of a hand, a beating heart, space opening out and time standing still . . . Quite an undertaking!

But to begin with, as in any study, we should define our frame of reference. Provided, of course, that our subject –

silence – will play ball. Because it's a slippery old customer that won't willingly allow itself to be pigeonholed, however inviting a pigeonhole it might be. So we should have a go at pinning it down . . . let's see what happens!

AN ATTEMPT AT DEFINITION

This morning, I was trying to remember the most silent place I'd ever been in my life. It was undoubtedly in Morocco – a dune in the Sahara that I visited a few years ago. With a group of friends, I'd got up before dawn to watch the sun rise. No wind, no sound, and red sand dunes as far as the eye could see. Since time immemorial, hermits and other seekers of the absolute have taken refuge in deserts. That morning, I realised why. Sitting alone on the sand, there was nothing more to do. Everything was there, simply as it was, without past or future. No need to run around aimlessly trying to prove something, chasing illusory successes or trying to catch comets' tails. Just take a deep breath and enjoy the moment's calm.

And then? And then the others arrived, shouting, 'Wow! It's so beautiful! Let's take a selfie!' and the magic melted away. Our awestruck faces were posted on Instagram #wearezen, and the desert sighed at such stupidity. As for me, I quietly stowed away a few grains of sand. And the sound of them rubbing together in my pocket acted as a reminder: the infinite is there, always available, to those who want to see it.

Silence has nothing to do with the absence of noise

Everyone has had this experience of the unlimited at some point: exploring a forest; stopping suddenly, immobile, in the midst of a moving crowd; travelling home on a bus in the middle of the night, listening to friends' conversations – at a distance – without really hearing them . . . Each time, silence was lying in wait. Between the words, between the usual images, between the familiar sensations, a parallel universe exists, one of absolute and nurturing calm. But the entrance to this world is jealously guarded by the sentinels of concentration and mindfulness. Because – let's be clear – silence has nothing, absolutely nothing, to do with the absence of noise.

That would be too simple. If all it took to enjoy silence and inner peace was to spend two hours a day in an isolation tank, we would know about it! These tanks were very fashionable in the 1970s and the trend has recently re-emerged in big cities, billed as a return to the womb. They're not recommended for the claustrophobic and are off limits for those on a budget, so in the following pages we'll focus instead on more poetic experiences that don't cost a penny.

But let's think about the human ear for a moment. According to scientists, it begins to detect sounds from 20 hertz upwards. So does that mean that the other frequencies don't exist? Spending a lot of time with cats and horses, whose hearing is extremely sensitive, I often find myself surprised to see them pricking up their ears when I can hear absolutely nothing. So I look confidently in the direction their ears are pointing and am greeted just moments later by the sight of a dog or someone out for a walk. Their auditory world is amazingly rich, and their quest for silence is probably very different from our own. Through frequent contact with these experts, I find myself frantically listening out in all directions, curious as to what I will hear. Hearing more connects me to the present moment and – ultimately – to silence.

Back in the heart of the city, I usually have to do the opposite: after spending hours developing the sensitivity of my hearing, it's quite difficult to return to the sonic cauldron of rush hour. At this point, as if by magic, my brain adopts a very simple, very effective technique: auditory amnesia. It forgets to listen in the city. It lets the sounds pass through the body without paying attention to them. This is a very practical solution, and what most people do to survive the cacophony surrounding them. Except when we are very tired, sounds mercifully only reach us through a filter, thanks to a sort of automatic aural desensitisation. Our ability to adapt is truly remarkable.

And the good news is that cities are also filled with silence and serenity. A subject we'll revisit a little later on.

Inner silence vs external silence

From the depths of silence, a little voice pipes up, 'What the hell are you waiting for? Tell them about inner silence!'

Although a little shocked by the impertinent tone of this little voice, I can't help but agree with it.

So, inner silence. That's the key. My thinking is based on the very simple principle that it's difficult to influence our environment, and the only lasting changes are those that depend on us and our own behaviour. You will perhaps be familiar with the famous lines from the Serenity Prayer that ask to 'grant me the serenity to accept the things I cannot change, the courage to change the things I can, and wisdom to know the difference'? So on the basis of this principle, if we can't get our neighbour to be quiet at 2 o'clock in the morning or stop our own children from making a racket when they're playing (or 'developing their creativity' as modern educationalists like to put it, probably not without a hint of sadism), what we can do is change our **perception** of the situation . . . or move house . . . or sell the children (oops, no, apparently that's illegal).

I want to explore the idea that the path of wisdom lies in the development of our inner silence, which will allow us to remain serene in tense situations, noisy environments or through emotional upheavals.

What is inner silence?

The notion of inner silence merits a little explanation. I'll be developing it at length over the following chapters, by studying various situations from everyday life, but here are a few pointers to begin with.

Let's return to the theme of the noisy neighbour. If you have an antisocial neighbour, you could use your inner silence to regain your calm by learning, for example:

- to let go of the mental images of your dear neighbour deliberately trying to ruin your life.
- to ignore the little voice inside you that says, 'I'm going to show him what I'm really made of!'.
- to study the feeling of anger, humiliation or impotence that appears in this type of situation and, having recognised it, allow it to subside by itself.

Once you've introduced these new strategies, a new internal rhythm can develop, a sense of calm more conducive to an enjoyable life. These exercises for learning to achieve inner silence involve our different domains of perception: the eyes, the ears (through words) and the body. For each of them, you will find specific examples to guide you, as well as a few little trade secrets, to test out in real life.

SOME BENEFITS OF BRINGING MORE SILENCE INTO OUR LIVES

There are many, many benefits. Allow me to mention a few here. Some are to do with our well-being, others with our social interactions, and others still relate to nothing short of world peace, on which more below.

Taking a step back and recentering yourself

Observing silence allows us to adopt a different, slower, more measured tempo in response to the agitation all around us. In the wake of the 2015 attacks in France, the media frenzy was perhaps more responsible for the general sense of anxiety than the events were themselves. We followed the arrest of the terrorists in real time across every TV channel, changed our Facebook profiles to 'Je suis Charlie' and endlessly commented on any tiny bit of news. In the weeks that followed, I received numerous requests for hypnotherapy from people suffering from a lack of sleep. They all shared the same profile: they had spent whole days glued to the TV and to news updates on their phones, so as not to miss the slightest shred of information. The images they had absorbed, the messages circulated over and over again on social media, had embedded themselves so deeply in them that it all formed a great black, terrifying cloud that was preventing them from moving on.

The situation would have been very different if they'd practised media silence: rationing the news, abstaining from social media for a few days, avoiding long, anxiety-inducing conversations – these are just a few suggestions for mental survival in the event of an upsetting news story such as this. The end result will be a reduction in stress, latent anxiety and the feeling of danger, as well as a lot less negativity flowing out into the world.

Deliberate silence and escaping from the agitation around

us means we can take a step back from the situation, preventing us from blindly following the media's analysis or that of other self-proclaimed experts, whose neutrality is often questionable.

The same rule applies in conflicts we might encounter at work, in our families or elsewhere. Observing silence means, for example, waiting before replying to a nasty email; perhaps leaving it overnight, or taking a deep breath before composing a reply: these approaches have the power to transform lead into gold!

A mission for the common good: contributing to world peace

World peace, no less. If you're going to have an ambition, you might as well think big!

So, world peace . . . Human beings often function by imitation. After a few minutes in the company of someone calm, we often feel our own internal rhythm changing as a result. Approaches to life are contagious, and keeping calm really is a mission for the common good. So from the bottom of our hearts, let's take this opportunity to thank those who each day decline to add their own voices to the cacophony around us. Those who don't state their opinion, those who let others speak, those who prefer a walk with their dog to a drink with friends and, last but not least, those who turn off the radio when they get in the car: these people are probably our 21st century saints.

THE VIRTUE OF SILENCE

I was recently invited to a cocktail party following an evening of lectures. Like everyone, I flitted from one group to the next to exchange a few words, catch up on their news and meet new faces. I talked to a lot of people that evening, and it was a real pleasure, but the conversations often resembled two monologues side by side rather than a genuine dialogue. During the evening, one of the speakers suggested a little game: the idea was to turn to the person beside us and hold their gaze for thirty seconds. Thirty seconds with a stranger is a long time! But I learnt more during that period of silence than in all the conversations that followed. Looking each other in the eye, slightly embarrassed at first, my neighbour and I plunged into the unknown, with no safety net. All of this in a room suddenly filled with a religious silence, punctuated by the odd burst of laughter.

This generates certain questions. How can I be with another person in silence? How can we be present in society without using words? How can I make my body manifest serenity and presence?

Answering these questions step by step can open the doors to a new way of being, allowing us to help build a better world.

'JUST A MINUTE' OF SILENCE

Nothing beats a little experiment to test the benefits of silence in real time. I don't know where you are right now as you read this: on a train (how delightful to be reading on the train!), in your bed, under a tree, in France, in America, in Thailand . . . But put down your book for a moment and look up. Look at the landscape, become aware again of your body, of your breathing, and stay there, doing nothing for a few seconds. Only sixty. Just a minute. And a much happier one than the melancholy minute of silence we share at times of national mourning. Poles apart, in fact: this is a self-willed minute's silence carved out of the passage of time.

It's over. The sixty seconds have passed. Did you notice? Time passes more slowly? Can you feel it? A different space opens up. Can you see? The contours of the world become sharper . . . and this is nothing compared to all the discoveries you could make by taking the odd pause in your daily life and looking up at the sky.

Our minute's silence seems to stop time. It's magic! And easier to feel when the body itself stays still. So try to practise these minutes of silence without moving: just be aware of anything changing or appearing.

THE SECRET

To really get into the experiment, the following meta-phor might help. Imagine you're on the motorway, driving at speed. The usual countryside rolls by, reas-suringly, with the odd bend here and there, but mainly the road is straight. Once on the motorway, you're safe. But there's a real risk you'll start to get bored. There's not much to see, the services are pretty grim, and inside the car it's starting to feel stuffy. What if you took the next exit? And took the time to explore a new road for a few miles? What if you took the risk of 'getting off the beaten track'?

A minute of silence carved out of our busy days is like that fun little detour from the monotonous straight road; it can change the tone of your whole day.

OVERCOMING OBSTACLES

Now it's time to get serious. Silence is golden, it's a fact, as all the sages and philosophers will tell us. So knowing this, what can be stopping us from bringing more silence into our lives? What is preventing us from offering up the sublime gift of our silence to the world? Because as we all know, we have 'the right to remain silent but anything we do say may be used against us'. And so? Why don't we use this right?

Let's be honest, there are numerous obstacles along the route to our Noble Silence. I've listed a few here, not to discourage you, but with the idea that it's better to know your enemy before going into battle.

In the meantime, a small digression: did you know that in the language of the Kogi people of Colombia, there is no word for 'enemy' or 'adversary'? An interesting thought in these troubled times of fierce ideological clashes. If the person in front of me is not an enemy but someone with a 'different system of thought', if the other person isn't an adversary, but someone with different values, there is nothing to fight and no one who stands to gain from my attacks. Another good opportunity for silence, perhaps . . .

Emptiness

DO YOU KNOW THAT FEELING OF EMPTINESS INSIDE?

Very often, silence frightens us. Especially these days, when we are bombarded with sounds, images and sensational news and stories. We are living in a cult of emotion, in which built-in obsolescence means our collective joys are short-lived, as we rush from one idea to the next . . .

Phew! It would be nice to be able to catch our breath. But to do so, we have to leave the path laid out in front of us to confront the greatest challenge that we can face in a human life: the feeling of emptiness. A few thousand years ago, the Buddha identified it as the source of human suffering; the sense of emptiness or dissatisfaction arising from any situation. Of course, this doesn't mean that emptiness, in itself, is negative or a cause of suffering, but that situations are *potentially* sources of this feeling of emptiness or dissatisfaction.

To put it another way, and paraphrasing the great French philosopher and mathematician Blaise Pascal, all our unhappiness stems from the fact that we cannot sit quietly and enjoy a summer evening with friends . . . without starting to take photos to post on Instagram. 'It's about sharing,' you'll tell me, and that's a noble intention. But let's take a moment to play back the scene in slow motion . . . It's 8.30 in the evening and you're sitting round the table with your friends. The atmosphere is upbeat, it's the weekend, and everything should be going well. So where does the need to document the moment come from, the nagging sense of restlessness that appears after a few minutes and has us reaching for our phones? Why can't we simply enjoy the moment? What needs to be added, and why do we feel something is missing? Is it more noise, more music, more alcohol, more friends, more atmosphere, more calm or more interesting conversations? What is it?

The actual Pascal quote referred to here is this: 'All of

our problems stem from one single cause, our inability to remain at rest in a room.'* Far be it from me to want to confine you to your bedsit, but the quote provides a marvellous illustration of the dissatisfaction or sense of emptiness that the Buddha described. You probably know what I'm talking about. An emptiness in the stomach or the solar plexus, a sense of incomprehension, a latent fear, an invisible threat . . . I won't go on with this description – it's unpleasant enough in itself, and you've probably already grasped what it is. So let's move on!

SITTING IN SILENCE TO OVERCOME THE EMPTINESS INSIDE

So what happens next? How do we escape from this feeling of emptiness?

The number one solution, which people have used since time immemorial, is to do something! We travel, go to the theatre, embark on passionate love affairs, have children, set up a business, and so on. All this to escape from our sense of emptiness. We have created a sort of society of distraction that takes us ever further outside ourselves. Everything seems designed to distance us from our true selves. Because if we ever stop for a moment and sit in silence, we will inevitably have to confront our feelings of emptiness . . . with no real idea of what to do.

....

* Blaise Pascal, *Pensées*, 1669.

Happily, there is a path that is beginning to emerge, and that path is **meditation**. Sitting down and facing (or rather sitting down *with*) these feelings of emptiness, but with a method to deal with them, of course (otherwise the experience would quickly turn into a nightmare). I'll be taking a close look at this approach over the following chapters.

DISCOVERING THAT EMPTINESS/EMOTIONS ARE IMPERMANENT

This is the key point in all these discussions: sitting down *with* our sense of emptiness and remaining seated alongside it is based on the principle that emotions are impermanent. Everything appears, and everything disappears, naturally. Everything. Emotions included. So long as we stop dwelling on them or feeding them. A recent experiment conducted at Stanford University once again demonstrated the significance of this. After attaching activity sensors to the heads of their volunteers, the researchers showed them different images to inspire feelings of fear, disgust or affection (pictures of kittens for this last one, no doubt!). They then measured how long it took the subject to return to his or her 'baseline' emotional state. So how long do you think an emotion lasts? A few minutes at most!

And yet, other emotions, like sadness, guilt or emptiness, are perceived as lasting much longer. And with good grounds, because we turn them over in our minds, dwell on them and gnaw on them like an old bone. If simply observed, an emotion – a void – will appear and disappear naturally. We leave it in peace, we accept its momentary existence, and calm appears.

It is this fundamental premise – that nothing lasts, emotions included – that will allow us to stay calmly seated when everything is in turmoil, and to master our silence.

Luminous solitude

I borrowed this phrase from a chapter in the Chilean writer Pablo Neruda's *Memoirs*, in which his travel impressions resonate, between the lines, with a sense of the joy of being alone*. 'Luminous Solitude' is a beautifully simple chapter, and one that I recommend you read – perfect to settle down with on a summer afternoon, your back resting comfortably against a tree. Silence and solitude certainly go well together, like two voices that combine to create a third, with infinite resonance.

For some people, being alone is the Holy Grail, the ultim-ate dream. I'm thinking particularly of busy mothers who have removed the concept from their vocabularies. 'On my own? Just reading or listening to music? Well, yes, when I was a student, but since then . . .' For others, solitude is something to shy away from: these are people who avoid

....

* Pablo Neruda, *Memoirs*, 2001.

their own company at all costs, for fear of sliding into despondency or melancholy. They are constantly going out, seeking adventures, in fact *anything* to avoid coming home to an empty house at the end of the day.

In either case – as always – it's all a question of perspective. One person shuts the door, takes off her shoes and sits down on the sofa with a sigh of happiness and relief. Another drops the kids off at school and relishes the slow walk back, savouring the calm . . . Both of them alone, in the light.

Silence likes to develop in solitude. By solitude, I mean the sensation of being connected to ourselves. Having the freedom, space and time to connect to our inner selves in a spirit of true friendship. It's about freely chosen solitude, a comfortable half-turn inwards with the power to nourish us before we return to the world. An intentional, coveted solitude in which we can learn much faster.

THE SECRET

It's sometimes enough to set aside a few hours with 'nothing to do', like stolen moments, in order to learn to be on our own and disembark on the sunny shores of our *true self*, which is much vaster than we could ever have imagined.

The three 'R's and four 'S's rule

I laughed a lot while learning this essential rule from my friend Salah-Eddine Benzakour – an international lecturer on the digital economy. The three 'R's and four 'S's are very simple: 'Repeat, Repeat, Repeat: Sounds Stupid but Secures Success.'* At the time, Salah-Eddine had the job of coaching me to give a TED talk, which has a very specific 'American-style' format. So we repeated, repeated, repeated . . . in order to achieve the desired result.

The three 'R's and four 'S's: 'Repeat, Repeat, Repeat: Sounds Stupid but Secures Success.' The whole of human wisdom – or almost – encapsulated in a single sentence! The brain learns by repetition. Actions or movements repeated a thousand times allow it to strengthen the connections between neurones.

So if you repeat the exercises in this book numerous times, the configuration of your brain will change. New inner pathways will gradually open out and flowers will spring up to line them. But that's not all! Our minds also work through 'branching', which means that everything is connected. So if we change one of our habits (looking at the sky more often, breathing from the abdomen or listening to the soundtrack of the world), our entire brain receives the feedback from this new behaviour. Like the cogs of a watch driving each other, or dominoes falling in a line . . . A little exercise changes the configuration of the whole system.

....

* Translator's note: the French original, 'Répéter, Répéter, Répéter : C'est Con mais C'est Comme Ça' has the edge over the English version thanks to its five 'C's compared to just four 'S's, as well as the fact that it contains a rude word!

'Repeat, Repeat, Repeat:
Sounds Stupid but Secures Success!'
'Repeat, Repeat, Repeat:
Sounds Stupid but Secures Success!'
'Repeat, Repeat, Repeat:
Sounds Stupid but Secures Success!'

This rule is probably one of the most important in the book. It takes a deliberate and sustained effort to change our mental habits and learn to connect to our inner silence at will. Think of the expressions 'Rome wasn't built in a day', and 'The longest journey begins with a single footstep' – the idea is simple: you have to practise the exercises frequently if you expect to get results. But rest assured, your efforts will be rewarded, even more than you can imagine. I strongly recommend choosing one or two exercises per day, plucked here and there from the pages of this book. Then after you've used the exercises to create new mental habits, your brain will go to work all on its own, so you won't have to exert yourself at all – just sit back and reap the rewards.

Silent inspiration

We're now setting out to discover different worlds, although their common denominator is a certain quality of silence, whether consciously chosen or not, in which we will find much to observe, learn and – I hope! – adopt in our own lives.

ANIMALS, MASTERS OF SILENCE

A strange place to meet

It was quite cold this morning: in this corner of the Alsatian Vosges that has been my home for the past sixteen years, the thermometer read -3°C. Following my daily routine, I put on my (vegan) fur coat, pulled on my boots, called for my two black cats and made my way to one of the huge meadows that surround the monastery. I went through the gate and stood there, at the top of the hill, calling out my rallying cry of 'Efstuuuuur!! Gazellaaaaa!! Come here my beauties!' The effect is not unlike the ululations you hear in North Africa, but after five attempts, I saw my two

Icelandic horses appear down below, approaching at a little trot. Quite a show, since they're both pretty laid back. So why the hurry? Because, like I do every day, I'd brought with me two bowls full of barley and 'OAP' special muesli to supplement their diets. A few months ago, they'd lost a lot of weight and I put them on a 'sumo' regime to help get them comfortably through the winter. Efstur and Gazella are the elders of the herd, although they're still in pretty good shape and full of life.

All around the monastery, along with the moles, martens, deer, crows, shrews, bees and so on, the meadows are home to around twenty Icelandic horses, owned by a charming couple who used to breed them. Having wound down their business, they are now letting their faithful steeds end their days in this little paradise. I do what I can to help, and keep a particular eye out for some of the horses, and Efstur in particular.

Efstur . . . In Icelandic, his name means 'supremacy' or 'the highest', and I have to say he wears it well! He's all white with a long mane and a very thick coat that means he can withstand the lowest temperatures. Icelandics live outside and gallop blissfully through the first cold snaps of winter. I could spend hours describing Efstur to you . . . but that's not what this book is about! It was he who chose me, a year ago. By that point, I was already taking care of the horses on a regular basis – grooming them, taking them for walks, or simply sitting down in their company. One fine day, Efstur started following me in the field. In the place where I used to meditate at the end of each afternoon, he sniffed the ground and walked nimbly round the log to stand behind me, with his neck over my head. It was summer, I was sitting on the ground, and his head became a lovely little parasol to protect me from the sun! Very practical, but my 'horse-parasol' was a little too unfocused for me to maintain the concentration required for meditation. The scene was repeated every day for a week. I ended up choosing another, quieter place in the forest to meditate, but since then, we've been inseparable!

Entering a new world . . . and learning to see things from a new perspective

Getting to know Efstur has taught me a lot. First of all, how to really make contact with someone else's world: in this case, 'someone else' is a four-legged creature with a mouth that is both enormous and . . . silent. As Prince Efstur did me the honour of making an approach, it seemed polite to try to understand his methods of communication and the way his mind works. When carefully entering another world, the hand that guides me is closer to that of the 20th century anthropologists than the explorers of colonial times. I approach with delicacy and curiosity, in a spirit of learning rather than obtaining, of understanding rather than imposing. And what a pleasure it is these days to be able to set off on an adventure . . . in the field next door!

Efstur doesn't speak. He's a horse, and the position of his

larynx makes any kind of speech impossible. And yet he communicates very clearly through his body language. His colleagues in the meadow understand instantly. At first, the message was more confused when it came through to me. During our early encounters, for example, I took the way he kept rubbing his head on me as his way of giving me a cuddle. I was so happy to get close to him and instantly receive these marks of affection. It was clear that Efstur adored me. Or at least that was my little human–animal analysis. The truth, when I discovered it, was much less romantic. After some animated discussions with Ute Weiland (the owner of the horses and an expert in equine behaviour), it turned out that this behaviour was about asserting control and expressing superiority: Efstur certainly does live up to his name! So I had to learn to push him back firmly at the slightest sign of dominance.

But the road was a long one. I was so keen to establish a relationship of trust based on mutual cuddles, complicity and gentleness, that the idea of having to impose my will on him disturbed me a great deal. Until the day when – wordlessly – I understood various things. If I didn't take the dominant role, Efstur would. There are no egalitarian relationships amongst horses: no referendums, unions or group therapy! In the equine world, there is a leader, full stop. And he is responsible for the safety of the herd. So on the one hand, I had to abandon my horizontal vision of the relationship (impose myself), and on the other, revise my conception of power (become the leader = major responsibility). A lot to absorb . . . and a complete para-digm shift.

In the world of horses, becoming the leader has nothing to do with showing your power, and is more a case of being at the service of the group. Naturally, the dominant horse goes first, eats first and demands respect, but there is a significant burden in exchange: he must permanently make sure he protects the herd. With Efstur, after much trial and error, I succeeded in establishing my dominance and in exchange I was able to offer him trust and put him at ease in any situation (even when the horse dentist visited, with some instruments that would make a GI quake in his boots, which is saying something!). And then when everything had become nice and clear between us, we raised our heads, pricked up our ears and trotted off together into the forest, snorting happily.

I learnt two things from this journey: to take control and to use that power for the good of the group . . . And a little bird tells me that the experience has been extremely educational!

So studying our fellow beings and their specific charac-teristics allows us to challenge many ways of thinking that had previously seemed set in stone. To open our minds and dare to change our opinions. Until I met Efstur, you might say I had specialised in an in-depth analysis of human rela-tionships. I enjoyed observing the human species and understanding individual personalities within the space of a few minutes, with or without the use of words. My template

THE GIFT OF SILENCE

was steeped in Freudian psychology, behaviourism and logical deductions, leading to a whole host of interpretations – with their fair share of unfounded projections: a subjective empiricism aimed at describing the world and conferring on it a logical framework. Reassuring, probably; misleading, most certainly.

An inner attitude based on silence and concentration

So how do we achieve this? How do we observe a horse, a group or an individual without projecting? For me, it all stems from adopting an inner attitude based on silence and concentration . . .

So with Efstur, I learnt to simplify, to look at just the facts. And to be extremely attentive.

But if you want to understand a principle, nothing beats a good example. Last week, I opened the gate to the meadow to take him out. He had the lead rope around his neck, because generally, he goes out of his own accord, ready for adventure. But this time, Efstur categorically refused to go through. He stood firm, placid, but at the same time, determined. I could have chosen any number of possible explanations: his legs hurt, he's playing up, he wants to test me . . . hard to tell. I could also have interpreted this 'song and dance' as a power play. And yet, I quickly and very simply realised that I should give up on the idea of taking him out. Just by seeing my horse's body language saying 'No!' so firmly that my own body sensed this 'No!' as if it were resonating from my head to my toes. To be able to hear a message like this, you absolutely must be physically present, focusing on the horse, rather than on your mental interpretations of the situation. An attitude of concentration and presence that allows you to 'simply receive information', in a sense (in this case, 'he really doesn't want to').

A little later that day, I found out that a few minutes earlier, another stallion had burst in on Efstur's herd of mares. So there was absolutely no question of him abandoning his beauties for a stroll in the forest. Of course, I could have made it a point of principle, by insisting and using force. In that case he would have followed me unwillingly and I would have won the battle. But that day, I chose instead to listen. To listen to the silent words of his body language. This time, the issue of dominance was irrelevant. And receiving Efstur's silent message and fully taking it on board resulted in a wonderful feeling of harmony between us. My understanding of that particular situation was made possible by the development of two states:

- **Inner silence**: the aim here is to ignore the habitual thoughts or logical reasoning that are constantly running through our minds. In Efstur's example, the following – logical – thought popped into my mind: 'Oh no my friend! I'm in charge and you're going to keep walking!' Considering the rules of natural horsemanship mentioned earlier (take the dominant role to make the horse feel secure), I should have heard this message and applied it.

But at the same time, the situation in itself and the horse's attitude were telling me something completely different. So I set aside the mind by completely ignoring my habitual thoughts, to put my trust in the conditions at that moment and my bodily sensations. To put it another way: I trusted Efstur, as a representative of Mighty Nature, rather than following rational pseudo-intelligence. At the point when I made this decision, the world filled with silence and the vast sense of calm that often appears when everything is in harmony.

- **Concentration**: horses can be extremely fast-moving and take you by surprise. When you're in contact with them, it's best to be truly present so that you can sense the slightest change in their rhythm or intentions. You need to concentrate on them with your eyes, ears and body, whilst remaining aware of the environment. A constant challenge! For example, I love to be in the middle of the herd in the meadows, sensing their shuddering, their breathing and their energy. Each horse is different, but they're constantly interacting. Sometimes, they'll suddenly gallop at full pelt from one end of the meadow to the other, kicking and bucking as they go. Such power and energy! At times like this, extreme concentration is required. That way, you can understand and merge into their world and even anticipate their movements. When you're with horses, past and future disappear to become an expanse of time filled with silence and presence.

Venturing further: abandoning well-trodden paths

So how can we maintain this concentration over long periods? When dealing with horses, it becomes absolutely necessary, as it must also always be when dealing with a wild animal. If my concentration wavers, all 400 kilos of Efstur could land on my foot, for example, because to be honest, my magnificent, pedigree prince is not always very dainty!

And how can we acquire and develop unwavering concentration in any given situation? The secret appears to lie in forgetting ourselves. And this idea can be taken far: forget other people watching us, forget the goal we want to achieve, forget what happened before in similar situations . . . Just focus on the action itself, on observing, on the task to be accomplished. And if your concentration should falter even slightly, don't waste a single second on regrets, simply return – immediately! – to the task itself. Just the horse, or the report to type up or the washing up to do. Feel your body: its position, your posture on the chair in front of the computer, your hands under the hot water, etc. This is the key to opening up a sensory universe . . . and the pleasure it brings with it. (See Chapter 5, 'Bodily Silence'.)

LALA THE CAT AND THE PRESENT MOMENT

But we're not finished with the animal kingdom just yet . . . The inspiration it provides deserves a whole book in its own right! And there are few sights more splendid than a cat washing itself. Each morning when I wake up, my mission is to feed the two little black balls of fur who share my life: Lala and Master Yoda (who is every bit as wise as his namesake). As soon as their meal is finished, they immediately lick themselves carefully clean from head to toe, in a specific order and with flexibility that would put even the most advanced yogi to shame. Front legs, back legs, belly, sides, face . . . everything is meticulously cleaned. So I've adopted the habit of getting up much earlier each morning to enjoy a cup of coffee as I contemplate their routine.

Sitting there with them, it's like watching a primitive dance: slow and untamed, performed to an age-old choreography. All of their concentration is focused on what they are doing at that point in time. Sometimes there are little pauses – if a noise captures their attention – but then they immediately go back to their business. There's an Olympian calm to their movements. Nothing is missing. And in fact, these early-morning performances send out a message that the most advanced Zen master would endorse: 'Concentrate! Apply yourself to your task with the same intensity!'.

'Intensity' is pretty much the perfect word to define this state of concentration we observe in cats cleaning themselves. But it isn't the only colour on my little feline Impressionists' palettes. At other times, an entirely different atmosphere of nonchalance permeates their lives. Their movements become languorous, with the odd bout of stretching, testing their claws on the wall, and so on. Everything slows down. Lala, my little black cat with the green eyes, is an expert at this.

And it's all the more remarkable because a moment later, she might leap from her bed with her fur bristling after seeing a shadow. But for the moment, there she goes, meandering her way towards her bed and patting down her cushions before yawning deeply. The mood is downright chilled . . . and so it's rest time. The Zen Buddhist master Taisen Deshimaru (1914–1982) expressed this idea in his own way in a piece of calligraphy with a crystal-clear message: 'It is sometimes useful to rest.' A few characters on a sheet of paper, and right in the middle, a big fat moggy having a snooze!

These different moments in the company of our cats (or dogs) certainly invite us to observe nature more closely. From nature, we can learn to receive messages of concentration, slowing down and respect for our natural rhythms. And to do this, a few days spent in the forest or the mountains can help a lot. Time changes, silence begins to unfold and some-thing else appears, beneath the surface.

But when our lives are caught up in the daily grind of eat-work-sleep, this is not always possible. So what should we do? Why not pay more attention to our cats, dogs or horses? And if you are not lucky enough to share your life with little (or large) travelling companions, why not watch some documentaries, read some books on animal behaviour or study the lives of your favourite animals? In my library, I have at least thirty books on animal behaviour, spanning everything from bees to wolves or pigs and, believe me, it's a fascinating subject. Besides the aspect of gaining knowledge, animals act as guides, helping us reconnect to the Earth. In our concrete cities, entering the wild world of a dog or a cat is perhaps a first step towards a necessary reunion with Nature that should be part of our daily lives.

> *To see a world in a grain of sand*
> *And a heaven in a wild flower,*
> *Hold infinity in the palm of your hand,*
> *And eternity in an hour.*

William Blake*

IN THE SILENCE OF A ZEN MONASTERY

If we were to encapsulate the 'silence of a monastery' in a single stereotypical image, it would show monks in single file, hoods over their bowed heads, walking slowly in line through the corridors of a Cistercian abbey. A vision of calm and solemnity. The image is admirable in every way and undoubtedly a source of inspiration. But because our Buddhist practice is open to the general public and has an entirely secular aspect, we present a very different face. First of all, our temple is mixed, the buildings are much more modest (as they must have been in the early days of Christian monasticism), the dress code is fairly free and slow movement is restricted to rest days.

....

* William Blake, 'Auguries of Innocence'.

Yet some mornings, when I'm changing the offerings of pure water on the altars in the monastery's various rooms, having leapt from my bed before dawn, I find myself moved by the thought of all the monks and nuns who have practised their spirituality in the shadows over the centuries . . . and who are still doing so to this day. In the early morning, with the night still shrouding each tree in its dark coat, I walk along the monastery's deserted avenues feeling the fleeting presence of fervent mystics of old who have preceded me in this quest. These are magical, timeless moments. The feeling that the unbroken thread of seekers of the absolute has woven an invisible lace, formed of prayers and mystery, that stretches up to that morning.

But if you feel a little alarmed by this lyrical outpouring, fear not: whilst newcomers on a retreat do have to rise early, they can limit their practice entirely to its secular aspect. Or to put it another way: mysticism is optional. For my part, it very quickly became the bedrock of my spiritual life, but many of my colleagues in the monastery have a much more down-to-earth and equally valid vision. The nature of Buddhist spirituality is that it ultimately adapts to the person who embraces it. The historical Buddha put it in these terms: 'Be your own light.' Nowadays we might say, 'It's up to you!'

So what is a Zen retreat like?

LEARNING TO MEDITATE

First and foremost, a Zen retreat allows people to discover the basics of the form of meditation we call *zazen*. This was the practice that enabled the Buddha to achieve enlightenment, sitting beneath the branches of the majestic tree under which he had taken refuge. A few thousand years later, millions of people around the world have adopted *zazen*, or seated meditation. And it seems that having reached the shores of Europe and the United States in the 1960s, meditation has enjoyed a second wind, spreading throughout society like a powder trail, albeit in a non-explosive form . . .

Human beings, caught up in the agitation of their frenetic lives, need silence and simplicity. Which is why these days many people enrol in meditation retreats at the various centres that have sprouted up over the past fifty years (see the 'Further Exploration' section at the end of the book). What they find there is an ordered, silent life, imbued with the values of thoughtfulness towards others, concentration and altruism.

So what actually happens in our monastery, in practical terms? It all begins at dawn, at around 6 o'clock. A monk runs through the buildings ringing a bell: this is the wake-up call! Everyone is asked to make their way to the dojo, or meditation hall. The daily timetable is strict and compulsory. No use thinking about whether or not we need to get up so early: we're expected for morning meditation without exception. It takes place in the half-light of the early morning, the magical moment when night gives way to day, gradually revealing the contours of the landscape. On arrival the previous evening, new participants will have received meticulous instructions from the monk or nun in charge of 'initiations': their immersion into the world of Zen! In the morning, participants have the regular rhythm of the monastery's large bell (weighing nearly 800 kilos) to help them in their meditation. It rings every two minutes, each time inviting us to renew our concentration. And concentration is the key word: as soon as the mind escapes, wanders back into last night's dreams or extracts itself from the present moment, as soon as we no longer know where we are and lose our awareness of our bodies, the deep, solemn resonance of the bell rings out as a reminder. In the incandescence of the early morning, we are immersed in the here and now.

RETURNING TO THE PRESENT MOMENT . . . THROUGH SILENCE

Days in the monastery are planned accordingly. Everything in the timetable is designed to allow you to reconnect with your body and the present moment. Meals, for example, are eaten in silence. This concept, unfamiliar to many, needs to be emphasised, and whilst the convivial spirit of dining with friends may be absent, those around the table can learn instead to taste and savour the food. The ingredients are organic and vegetarian, whilst the little chant at the beginning of the meal invites us to offer thanks to every element involved in bringing the food to the table. So we invoke the sun, the rain, the cook and the people who grew the vegetables, all equally: a fairly long and unbroken chain of contributors to our monastic feast. This is also the time to think of the many people who are not lucky enough to get enough to eat, and to vow to make the best use of the energy provided by the meal: plenty of food for thought!

Silence is a key element of the retreat. Some retreats are conducted in total silence, but most simply offer periods of silence of various lengths at certain points of the day. Meditation, meals and work for the community are all conducted in silence. These alternate with opportunities for dialogue, when you can happily chatter away. This alternation gives the days a harmonious rhythm and makes the retreats more accessible to newcomers. In the beginning, it's great to be able to discuss your experience. Because when it comes down to it, retreats are a major commitment: one activity follows another, meditation is sometimes hard, and personal time is reduced to the minimum. So these windows of 'non-silence' work a bit like decompression chambers, allowing you to gather your strength in order to surpass your limits. A bit like the Buddha's beloved Middle Way!

For the more advanced, fully silent retreats are also held several times a year. I admit that I appreciate these days of calm in particular. According to the Tibetan science of energy, the total absence of words has the benefit of 'clearing the subtle channels'. Words and ideas left unsaid disappear, purely and simply, allowing for a process of purification. After a few days of silence, you can easily sense the results of this inner cleansing: everything becomes simpler, mountains turn into mounds of earth and storms into spring breezes. And all this thanks to silence. It allows us to truly be *with* things, in direct contact, without the filter of the mind. In silence, during a retreat, we feel the resonance of the great bell pass through our bodies; we notice the delicacy of a bird hopping through the snow for the first time; a fly buzzing through the air is truly heard.

LEARNING TO BE MOVED

After three days of a retreat (the usual format of *sesshins*, or Zen retreats), most people say that the scales have fallen from their eyes: they have rediscovered their sight or, in Buddhist terms, 'deep vision'. What an adventure! Despite the fact that the activities over those days have been extremely simple: sitting, eating, giving thanks, chopping vegetables, sleeping . . . Yet it is as if the contours of the world have come into focus, giving everything more texture and light. It may not be that the world has changed, as such, but through meditation the participants have regained the capacity to see and to be moved. The proof is there on their faces. On arrival, some have rings around their eyes and heavy limbs. The traditional group photograph at the end of the retreat always shows radiant faces, bright eyes and relaxed features.

But there's no denying it, a *sesshin* is not easy. This is due to the body staying immobile for long periods of time, but is also because of all the emotions that pass through us. Peaceful joy only appears after you have negotiated the shadows. And the retreat very often resembles the classic 'hero's journey'. Everyone will go through some sort of test (aching knees, overwhelming anger, loss of patience . . .), encounter a dragon to slay, find their own inner resources, be faced with a battle and have a princess or prince to save before – finally! – the serene knight is crowned with a laurel wreath.

As I'm writing these words, nice and cosy in a popular café in Strasbourg, I overhear a conversation. A little family group has sat down a few metres away from me and are eating a local speciality, *tarte flambée*, topped with another Alsatian favourite, pungent Munster cheese! There's the grand-father, the mother and her son of about ten. The grandfather has borrowed his daughter's phone to call one of his other children: 'We're thinking of you. We're eating a *tarte flambée* and we're really thinking of you. It's snowing here. Have you put your snow tyres on?' I find this dialogue moving and wonderful. The human capacity for emotion is inexhaustible, and these are the sort of tender feelings we reconnect with during Zen retreats.

Longer, or even very long-term retreats

The monastery was founded in 1999, and some people have been there since the beginning, which makes all the difference. Eighteen years of communal life, beneath the starry skies of a spiritual life, forges a very special connection between people. And silence plays a key part, providing the perfect setting.

PEACE IN THE MIDST OF PASSING TIME

When you have vowed to share your daily life with other monks and nuns, and will be seeing their cheerful or frowning features morning to night, it's a good idea to learn some diplomacy. And above all, learn to button your lips. At the beginning of my experience of this, we were perhaps childishly enthusiastic about our 'cohabitation' and tried to say everything, change people, or even devise strategies to assert our own vision. In those early days of the community, we had our fill of talking at great length, comparing notes, complaining and locking horns. Occasionally someone might even have spent a few days sulking, endlessly mulling over futile grievances that good sense – had it deigned to make an appearance – would have treated with contempt, so as not to waste time.

After all these years, experience has taught us that 'useful' conflicts rarely arise. And that most of our griping is pointless. And so monks and nuns live together in consensual silence, in a pledge of harmony. Of course, there's the weekly meeting to raise some point of disagreement or other, exchange a few words on the necessity of buying new plates (I'm quoting here!) or changing the serving arrangements, a few outbursts – sometimes, when people are tired – which are quickly calmed and above all soon forgotten. So on a day-to-day basis, everyone makes an effort to leave things unsaid: reproaches, personal concerns, potential meltdowns, etc. The general atmosphere is at stake, and the presence of numerous newcomers each week encourages this reserve.

This approach allows things to calm down much more quickly. We let conflicts pass by – where possible – in the same way as we do with thoughts and emotions during meditation. Our shared history, all those years spent together, has taught us that it is possible to put great trust in the impermanence of things and the capacity of situations to settle down by themselves. I have probably 'had words' with most of the monks and nuns in the monastery. At certain points, our visions of the world have clashed, with neither side able to drop their guard. How long would these episodes last? For as long as a rose is in bloom . . . for an instant. And each time, willingness or simply the passage of time have made reconciliation possible. This knowledge alone is extremely precious. It is possible to learn to live together!

The rule of silence, whilst recommended, is not absolute, however, and at the monastery there are numerous opportunities to talk, when necessary. It is sometimes very useful to be able to 'unload' when the burden is too heavy. During *dokusan* (individual interviews with the abbot), for example, when words can be unburdened freely. They then stay behind in the room, as if released, and we go away relieved, very often having forgotten the problem that brought us there.

TOGETHERNESS IN SILENCE

The residents of a monastery can be of any age and come from all social backgrounds. It's a place that brings together different worlds that would probably not cohabit on the outside. The Ryumonji monastery, for example, is currently home to a saxophone teacher, a traveller who has been around the world, a secretary, a nurse, a classroom assistant, a plumber, a psychology student, a TV actress, an IT student, a mathematics researcher, a software programmer, a telephone counsellor for the drugs information service, a company boss, a machinery salesman for the food processing industry, a film voice-over . . .

What a Tower of Babel! And yet they are not brought together by their labels (their roles in society) but by meditation and spiritual values. Whilst someone's career is sometimes briefly mentioned, it is through everyday actions that we get to know other people. Beyond words, through their behaviour and attitudes. So we develop a genuine togetherness, based on the utmost respect. And by paying a little attention, we gradually get to know and respect our limits and fragilities. This approach means people accept each other in silence and compassion, and allows a genuine group spirit and spiritual community to emerge.

THE GIFT OF SILENCE

You can easily adapt certain details of this monastic environment to your everyday life, in your own home: planning periods of digital detox, observing a few minutes of silence before eating (or even eating lunch in silence), opening the bedroom window when you wake up to savour the atmosphere of the day, and so on. A little further on in the book (and particularly in Chapter 5), you will find some very practical ideas for introducing little pockets of the silence and serenity found in a monastery into your home and daily life.

PART TWO

Silence in all its guises

3

Visual silence

VISUAL POLLUTION AND
THE ALL-POWERFUL SCREEN

Our eyes in the city

A few years ago, I rented a little pied-à-terre in Strasbourg in order to divide my time between the monastery and city life. Three days in town, four days in the country, a perfect way of not having to choose between being either a town mouse or a country mouse. This interlude lasted five years, during which one of the most important lessons I learnt was the difficulty of juggling two homes, forever emptying and filling suitcases. But that's another story . . .

In Strasbourg, the 'Capital City', as it's known, I lived in a small district popular with students, a stone's throw from the famous cathedral and right by the river that winds its way lazily through the city centre. The historic houses, the riverbanks dotted with students from the early hours, the bars on barges . . . all this gave the place a very nice little bohemian vibe.

And yet this was the place where I became aware of something that has become very commonplace in our lives, so natural that we could even forget it exists: visual pollution! Leaving my flat, whether I turned left or right, my eyes were inexorably drawn to a choice of shops, advertising hoardings, neon signs lit up day and night, etc. The essence of the subliminal message being permanently broadcast in all directions was: 'Consume us', 'Buy us . . .', 'Take us!' I felt as though I was in *The Jungle Book* under the spell of Kaa the snake. Or rather under the influence of thousands of snakes with bulging eyes all trying to hypnotise me. In circumstances like that – which you can easily envisage – remaining focused and in the present moment is an extremely difficult task.

Because, setting aside the simplistic premise that all this shopping would actually make me happy, the most noticeable effect of this profusion of advertising was to permanently draw me 'out of myself'. With each sign, a visual stimulus was asking my brain to make a decision: yes, no, later, why not? With each advert (underwear, telephone, energy drink . . .), the same thing: in a fraction of a second, my brain had to decide what to do with the information. Would it wonder whether it was actually time to change my phone? Evaluate the condition and performance of the old phone? Think about the different contracts? And so on. And most of the time all this goes on entirely subconsciously.

In practical terms, instead of walking peacefully through the city, enjoying the vibe, I found myself moving mechanically, as if held on a leash by invisible threads of light connected to the advertising hoardings and shop windows. The positive side of this consumerist hypnosis is always the same: a distraction from reality, and the possibility of escaping into the world of dreams and imagination in order to scrupulously avoid having to confront potential emotional disturbances (see Chapter 1, 'Emptiness'). But the negative side, which certain spiritual masters – understandably – have no hesitation in describing as tragic, is this: by allowing my saucer-like eyes to direct my steps, I have become . . . a robot!

The challenge of our screens

And that's not all.

(Note to the reader: as a natural optimist, I'm not in the habit of drawing up a whole list of negatives or enumerating the dysfunctional aspects of society like a harbinger of doom. In this case, however, it seems to me that mentioning these facts in concrete terms can help us gain a better understanding of the challenge we face. And since the point of a challenge is to rise to it, once the diagnosis has been made, you'll find in a few pages' time some quite effective remedies to escape from this 'collective hypnosis': I promise!).

So that's not all. Inside our homes as well as outside, in town and in the country, we're now caught in an invisible net: a net cast by all the different screens surrounding us.

The paradox this time is that we're simultaneously the fly and the spider: voluntary prisoners in a web we've spun ourselves, or at least been happy to help finance. My aim here isn't to argue for or against the internet, or for or against smartphones, tablets and other digital delights. Given that I'm writing this book on a laptop connected to the internet, it would be hypocritical at the very least to be promoting a return to the Stone Age by banning these offending objects. On the contrary, our spiritual and philosophical path leads us more in the following pragmatic direction: learning WITHIN situations rather than avoiding them. Or to put it another way: what can we do under our current given circumstances?

But first of all, a question: what happens when we automatically skip from one screen to another, from tablet to television to smartphone, all day long? Various things. We forget where we are, for example. We 'lose' our body or the sensation of having a body. We're caught up in a virtual reality that, far from making us happy, very often stirs up our frustrations and emotional fragilities. All the horrors that the world can produce stream into our wide-open eyes without any filters. And the occasional images of cute little kittens cuddling up to baby piglets can't counteract the sight of a toddler's bloody face amidst the bombing in Aleppo.

So the omnipresence of screens generates a sort of agitation inside many of us. A feeling of stress. Messages continually pour in via email, Twitter, Instagram or

Snapchat. In order to maintain the artificial cocoon of the network, the feeling of belonging to a group or the illusion of being someone special, they all demand an almost immediate response. What's more, from the point of view of regular brain function, unprocessed information is left 'hanging', as if in a queue, fairly quickly coming to resemble the notorious queues for shops in the old Soviet Union. But there's nothing like a concrete example to illustrate my point: I'm busy writing this book, when my mailbox starts flashing red to show that I've received a new email. I open it almost unconsciously and find an urgent message asking me for a photo of the last retreat of the summer to be sent asap to the International Zen Association (a genuine example). I get back to my work, with a part of my mind occupied by this task that will have to be dealt with at some point. After ten similar episodes, twenty super-interesting-videos-to-add-to-my-favourites-and-watch-later and thirty desperately urgent messages asking for information on meditation, my brain is saturated! Ring any bells?

The common thread to all these episodes is that they take us out of ourselves. Screens – large or small – have an unparalleled power to fascinate. Like a whole host of 5,000-watt mindfulness vacuums, able to capture the attention of the most battle-hardened Zen master. Their lure is very powerful! But we haven't yet said the final word on this . . .

CONTROLLING OUR GAZE: WHY AND HOW

Writing these few lines, I'm happy to see that my reflexes for returning to the present moment, which I have patiently developed over the course of the last few years, are bearing fruit. They're based on very simply physiological principles, which are permanently accessible and, best of all, free (something that is rare enough these days to be worth pointing out!).

Why should we control our gaze?

One of the common themes shared by light pollution and the omnipresence of screens is their ability to take hold of us and draw us outwards. To grab our attention and introduce the aforementioned sensation of emptiness or latent dissatisfaction into the background of our lives, this sort of almost permanent agitation inside us. This puts our mind into 'hyperactive mode' or 'stress mode', as it desperately searches outwards for the magic solution to our inner unease.

Luckily, it is possible to calm this mental strobe light in the space of a few minutes. All these light signals, whatever form they take, are received through our eyes. So learning to rest the eyes, to control our gaze in order to regain control of ourselves, is an extremely constructive and valuable exercise.

What to do with our eyes in the city

There are different ways to navigate a city. The one I'm suggesting here is a kind of walking meditation, at your own normal pace. The key concept is to take back control of your eyes in order to regain control of your mind. After a few minutes, you will have enjoyed the benefits of a walk, without the accompanying commercial hypnosis, and your mind will be significantly more peaceful, I promise.

'CONCENTRATING' YOUR EYES IN AN URBAN ENVIRONMENT

You can use this exercise anywhere and, given that we often find ourselves walking around our cities or towns (going to work, to university, going shopping or meeting friends for a coffee), more importantly you can use it often – as often as possible, so as to introduce new behavioural habits that reconnect you to reality. So how does it work?

1. First of all, focus on it when you leave the house: reminding yourself of the incredible rewards this will bring, for example, or simply telling yourself,

in reaction, that no, you are not a robot! Next, set off on foot whilst resting your eyes, in other words deliberately controlling the direction of your gaze. Knowing exactly where you're looking at the point at which you look. Deliberately choosing to avoid a certain sight, shop window, person, etc.

This practice, which is also described in numerous spiritual traditions, is known as 'concentration'. It naturally requires training.

2. Do this regularly for around 5 minutes during your journey. Take note of the occasions when your attention wanders and what it is that attracts your gaze elsewhere. Becoming aware of what grabs your attention is extremely interesting! It's a wonderful tool for self-knowledge, freeing you up from any preconceptions.

At the beginning, the exercise can seem difficult, especially when you become aware, like other urban meditators before you, of the speed at which the mind wanders. Don't worry: this is normal! And concentration can be learnt quickly, in small steps.

To make things easier, try to look downwards at

first to help calm your gaze. Things down there might seem less interesting . . . unless you find poetry in a cigarette butt, or like to make out pictures in puddles. But usually looking downwards, a few metres in front of you, helps you to cut yourself off from the visual messages, and to recentre yourself more easily.

CALMING THE GAZE:
VISUAL PAUSES

The mind–body connection

The connection between the mind and our physiology is already established. The body influences the mind and vice versa, as you'll be able to experience in a few moments. This might seem insignificant but it's an essential truth in any search for knowledge, whether in terms of personal development or the most profound spirituality. Working on the body, for example, is the way that Indian yogis or practitioners of Japanese shugendõ deepen their intuitive knowledge of reality. The former visualise a fire and are able to stand barefoot in the snow by means of impeccable concentration. The latter practise under icy waterfalls, developing an uncommon degree of mental strength.

THE GIFT OF SILENCE

There's also a little anecdote that has done the rounds in Buddhist circles, illustrating the power of thought over the mind and, naturally, encouraging people to use it wisely. It goes like this: a man gets into a refrigerated lorry in England to clean it. The doors accidentally shut, and the lorry sets off on a long journey across Europe, with the man trapped inside. When the driver opens his doors in southern Spain, he discovers a rigid corpse. The man has frozen to death. Except, and this is the point of the story, the refrigeration system wasn't working!

So the body influences the mind but also our state of mind, and acting on the body can rapidly alter our moods.

Important information: the eye exercise below goes far beyond its apparent simplicity. It is an essential, primordial technique. You could practise it over the next fifty years (let's be optimistic) and discover something different each time. It entails letting go completely and gives you an instant check-up on your current inner state. It was already described in the magical writings of the ancient spiritualities and contains the wisdom of several millennia. It opens the doors to a new form of perception that poets have embroidered upon at length.

Beware! The exercise below has the power to touch your heart . . . To move you deeply . . . Take a deep breath . . . Are you ready?

THE VISUAL PAUSE EXERCISE

A little bit of advice: when I introduce this exercise to a group, people often ask if they can close their eyes. It would probably be more comfortable like that, of course. But the aim of the exercise is to recentre ourselves whilst maintaining – and this is important – the most tangible possible contact with reality. If you close your eyes, there's a serious risk of quite quickly finding yourself lost in your thoughts and daydreams . . . This is no help when you want to discover your inner silence in a state of full consciousness of the present moment!

• Sit down somewhere calm, even in front of your computer as long as it is switched off. Adopt an upright, energetic, motivated posture, like an explorer setting off to discover the new world. Remember to place both feet on the ground to keep your connection to the Earth and help you to develop your bodily presence.

THE GIFT OF SILENCE

- Look a few metres in front of you, with your eyes directed diagonally downwards.

- Let the muscles of your eyes gradually relax: your eyelids, around the eyes, behind the eyes. At the beginning, you're sure to feel a great tension in the eyes, which has to do with the intense mental activity of our modern world. This is not a problem and entirely normal at the outset, simply take note of it. It is also a necessary step towards something else . . .

- After a few minutes, the gaze relaxes. The cheek muscles join in with the relaxation movement, along with the whole of the face. You adopt a neutral attitude inside, without expression, or any particular desire.

The phenomenon of clinging

The eyes are connected to what we call 'clinging', or the desire to obtain something. This is an energy that exists in the background of our lives. We can feel the power of our clinging for example when we're – finally! – on holiday. After working for weeks to pay for this fantastic holiday, dreaming about the moment when we'll finally be able to stretch out blissfully on the soft sandy beach, by the turquoise water, with a warm sun playing on our backs, here we are! Sitting on the beach towel looking out at the iridescent water. But our happiness is short-lived. We've barely had the chance to savour the moment when our brains start whirring, in search of something else: it's too hot, the sand is irritating our skin, we're thirsty, we really must take some photos to post on Instagram, we've forgotten our sunglasses, we want to dive in, we're scared of sharks . . . A sort of permanent dissatisfaction, discontentment or sense of emptiness that appears spontaneously in everyone (see Chapter 1).

So to appease this discontentment, we grasp at things, we have this desire for appropriation, movement, change. We change position, we order a cocktail, we turn over and over on our towels, we go for a swim, we look to the left and to the right at the other members of our beachside community to distract ourselves, etc. In the whole of this process, the eyes play a central role. Each time we look for something outside ourselves, they tense up. A tiny, but very real, tension from seeking the solution to our inner discontentment in the outside world.

Whereas, in short, we simply need to rest our eyes to calm our inner tension! The exercise is so simple that I almost didn't dare suggest it, imagining the reader's reaction. 'Who's she trying to kid? Just rest my eyes and all my problems will be solved?!' And yet this awareness, with its power to bring about major changes of perspective, really is that simple. Sit down somewhere peaceful for a few moments and . . . have a go!

THE BENEFITS OF SIMPLICITY

During a retreat in Japan about ten years ago, I was struck by the art of simplicity, but above all by the well-being it generates. Conditions in the monastery in Nagoya were extremely harsh (no heating, cold water on every floor, all living cheek by jowl . . .) and the little nuns, Zen as they might be, had the knack of testing me to the limit. Kept busy from morning to evening, I rushed around the corridors not always sure what was going on, trying above all not to be a nuisance. As a westerner, I'd been accepted with a lot of reservations, because most of the teaching was in Japanese . . . but the magic of the place and the profound wisdom it exuded made all the challenges disappear.

One afternoon, one of the nuns took me to the private tea room, where the venerable 85-year-old abbess, Shundo Aoyama, received her distinguished guests. My task was to dust the room meticulously, attentive to each movement, focusing on my cloth as if it were the most precious stone. After a few minutes, looking away from the table I was polishing for a moment, I suddenly found myself right in front of an alcove standing 180cm tall and 60cm wide, a sort of niche in one of the walls of the room. The alcove was empty, with the exception of a little statue of Kannon, the goddess of Compassion, with her thin, elongated physique, stretching delicately up towards the sky. Although minuscule, the goddess seemed to emanate a gentle light in all directions. There was no other decoration in the tea room: nothing besides this alcove and the little statue, a tiny presence in the large niche. I had the feeling of receiving a secret teaching, which sometimes reveals itself to those who can see it: the lesson of the serene beauty of empty space.

The arts in Japan have developed over several centuries in this minimalist vein, inspired by the Zen tradition. Starting from the principle that décor and the environment have an immediate impact on our state of mind, don't we take inspiration from this to calm down our visual space? Tidy away, empty, throw away surplus objects. Why not give away, sell or donate what we no longer need? And treat our eyes to the luxury of empty space! A freely chosen emptiness, synonymous with wisdom and tranquillity, in which open space can once again spread its wings, as we also spread ours.

FACE TO FACE WITH OUR MENTAL IMAGES AND LEARNING TO LET GO

When I started meditation, I was taught various things about the posture to adopt, my breathing and my thoughts. The most common advice on this last subject was: 'Let your thoughts go by like little clouds in the sky.' This always confused me. In the beginning, when I started out, my thoughts were more like a tower of great storm clouds than fluffy little sheep, and this really left me feeling helpless. But above all, there were two essential things that I needed to know: what are thoughts? And most importantly, how can we 'let them go by'?

Over long hours of practice, I quite regularly caught myself secretly grumbling whilst the master pronounced, with the confidence of someone who knows exactly what he's talking about, 'As soon as a thought appears, let it pass by, without doing anything . . .' To which my bolshy little inner voice would reply, 'Fine, OK, we know! But how?!' Anyway, before I went crazy or turned into the worst sort of professional moaner, I set about seriously studying the issue. I turned to the neurosciences and their – fairly recent – research into the workings of our consciousness, but also approached the subject via altered states of consciousness, like hypnosis. It was during my hypnotherapy training at the Académie Arche (in Paris) that I discovered a simple classification of 'thoughts' that made my task a great deal easier.

'Silence on set': the content of our thoughts

Well no, I'm not about to reveal the detailed content of my thoughts! Partly because the children aren't in bed yet, and partly because there's something much more interesting to discuss: the structure or the form of our thoughts. In Buddhism, they are also known as mental objects, an object being something you can place in front of you in order to study it. Turning the content of our minds into physical objects makes it easier to observe. In technical terms, for those who want to impress people at dinner parties or corporate meditation seminars, this is known as 'metacognition'. In Buddhist terms, the concept is taken a bit further still, opening up the mystical possibility of a 'thought with no thinker', a theory that has become entirely plausible in light of recent advances in research into the brain, which in answer to the crucial question, 'So where does consciousness come from?', reluctantly offer a 'dunno'.

So to sum up: what do we mean by 'thoughts'? Or to put it another way, 'What is this stuff inside my head?'. In simplified terms, thoughts can take three forms: images, sounds or physical sensations.

In this chapter on the subject of silence and the eyes, we'll be looking at images. When we think or let our minds gently wander, our thoughts often take the form of visual images: like a little film reel playing automatically inside us. With an amazing range of subjects and a director who often seems to have ingested some illicit substances. So we can jump from one image to another with no apparent link: we begin by thinking about our shopping list (with a visualisation of the products, the list itself, or the aisles of the organic shop we usually visit . . .), but then a fraction of a second later we move on to our plans for the afternoon (visualisation of the different places or a page from our diary), taking the car for its MOT, etc. And that's just the visible part of the iceberg, which is already pretty chaotic. But actually, if we observe our thoughts with even more concentration (in meditation, for example), visual thoughts very often look like little snippets, lightning-fast images: a flash of light or a scene, successive images, memories, etc. It's worth noting

77

that studying this content will reveal treasure troves of creativity in every one of us, with all sorts of potential applications: the visual arts, of course, but also new projects, decoration, cookery, etc. (that was to motivate you to do the exercises . . .).

But thoughts, as we'll be discussing at length in the next chapter, can also take the form of auditory content: these can be sounds we've heard that are instantly reflected in our brains, but most importantly – by some distance – the almost permanent resonance of our internal dialogue, aka 'the little voice in our heads'. There's a lot to say about this, especially if – like mine – this internal dialogue is a freewheeling affair, like a cyclist hurtling down the Alpe d'Huez in the Tour de France! (To be continued in Chapter 4).

Finally, the third type of 'mental object', or the third possible form taken by this succession of thoughts moving past 'like little clouds in the blue sky', consists of the physical sensations and emotions we feel within our bodies (more about this in Chapter 5).

A few little games to play with your brain

So now this has been explained, what do we do to introduce or encourage some inner silence? Or to put it another way, 'turn off the TV for a while'? There are a range of possibilities. The first stage consists in making ourselves aware of the content of our mind.

BECOMING AWARE OF YOUR 'INTERNAL FILM SHOW'

For thousands of years, sages of all kinds have accomplished this by sitting still and in silence. It would appear that slightly distancing ourselves from the usual sensorial whirlwind and going somewhere quiet is a great help when it comes to introspection. It certainly seems logical, and on our path towards wisdom we may as well imitate the experts! So a calm place to observe ourselves thinking. Ultimately, this observation will be possible anywhere, and in fact is highly recommended everywhere, as a way of showing us in real time what we're thinking 'up there' inside our skulls.

I should point out, however, that this rule of silence and immobility has been challenged with great elegance by certain 'wandering' philosophers, such as the great German philosopher Heidegger, who found walking to be the ideal state in which to connect himself to his thoughts. (Were they mental images? We may never know, but – without wanting to put any psychics out of business – I would plump for Heidegger's mental universe being more of the 'inner dialogue' type.)

Once you're sitting still, close your eyes for a moment or look in front of you, down towards the ground. This will help you to gradually relax your gaze, which, as we've said, will decrease the number of images that appear. But that isn't the aim of the exercise. The idea now is to go in search of your brain, and its contents, which will be surprising to say the least. Point the spotlight and observe the images, colours and forms that appear: a whole world suddenly opens out in front of you!

THE SECRET

To observe, you have to find a vantage point, in other words a space from which to observe. This we describe as 'mindfulness', the 'witness state' or 'observational awareness'. My first Zen master, Olivier Reigen Wang-Genh, talks about 'full presence', which has the advantage of involving the whole body in the observation, and entirely corresponds to our experience of it. Here's the thing: you don't use your head to observe your head! You will need to find another perspective and create some more distance.

For my part, it took several years – five, in fact – for this to become possible, due to the numerous obstacles in my path: uncontrolled emotions, fears and a real lack of confidence in my abilities. These different things took up all the space inside, and I was unable to extricate myself from them. So in parallel, I began some extremely interesting psychotherapy work before turning to hypnosis and self-hypnosis.

During my first, fairly faltering years of 'observation of my inner film show', when I felt I was slightly swimming through fog, I also felt that things were gradually settling, like a mist that clears over the fields in the early morning. The sun that warmed the fields inside me was the regularity of these periods of sitting in silence. At the monastery, each morning and each evening, the community gathers in the dojo for *zazen*, seated meditation. Whether it's raining, windy or snowing, the timetable is set in stone, and the body itself seems to be expecting these moments of calm that give the days their rhythm.

PLAYING WITH MENTAL IMAGES

I was very interested to discover this exercise during my studies of hypnosis and neuro-linguistic programming (NLP). It's more interventionist than the previous exercise and encourages you to work directly on the contents of your mind rather than simply observing them. So from a Buddhist and therefore spiritual point of view, we are remaining IN the mind, rather than attaining 'Full Presence'. The head working on the head, in a sense. But far be it from me to discredit this practice or conceal its benefits! Working on mental images is very, very effective and something I teach my hypnotherapy patients every day.

The underlying idea is extremely simple: our inner world is a representation of the external world, dependent on our means of perception. So if you put two people in the same place in front of the same landscape, their mental images of it will differ significantly according to the way they are in the habit of receiving information. One person, with a fairly dreamy, laid-back disposition, might look at the sky. The other, a retired farmer, say, will look at how the fields are being farmed. If you want to explore this idea more deeply, you could study Schopenhauer's book *The World as Will and Representation* (*Die Welt als Wille und Vorstellung*), which deals with these mysterious questions . . . and many other equally fascinating subjects.

And once you've put the book down, back to the exercise!

As with meditation–observation, find somewhere quiet for the first few times. Close your eyes and look inwards at your mental images (without making yourself cross-eyed!). To bring a little peace to this world entirely constructed by your unconscious, begin by slowing down the pace at which the images appear. Imagine that all these images are weightless, for example, or like a film playing in slow motion, shot by shot. You can be the projectionist of your own film and control the equipment. You can adjust the film's settings using a magic remote control to . . . anything is possible! In this way, you can gradually introduce periods of silence, or relative tranquillity, into your mental universe. A very good way to fight stress!

THE SECRET

The meditation–observation exercise on page 79, *becoming aware of your 'internal film show'*, familiarises you with these mental images. So it's a good idea to begin with a few minutes of silent observation, like a sort of check-up, before working on the contents of the mind.

(4)

Verbal silence

Of all those who have nothing to say, the most agreeable are those who do it in silence.

Nicolas de Chamfort*

I 've always loved to natter, babble, rabbit on . . . A complete chatterbox! Even at primary school, I was quite an animated child, and the warnings rained down on me: 'A gifted pupil, but leads her classmates astray', 'Good results, but watch the behaviour!', etc. It was also at this point that – on the suggestion of my enlightened teacher, Mrs Geneviève Deverain – my parents signed me up for a hatha yoga course, in an attempt to calm me down a bit. In the early 1980s, courses like that were quite rare, yoga being nothing like as popular as it is today. I was very lucky, because what I learnt was enormously beneficial and certainly contributed to the spiritual direction I took later on. In spite of all this, at 7 or 8 years old, I was a real gas-bag!

....

* The eighteenth-century writer known for his witty maxims.

Little changed over the next few years, and it was only much later that silence offered itself up, as a pleasure. More than a pleasure, in fact: there's a profound contentment to be found in not saying anything. In a group, my words can come thick and fast as we discuss different topics. But mostly, staying silent and observing has become THE absolute luxury. This syllabic calm is something I savour – in the city or in the forest – while realising how lucky I am. This development came about through a number of steps: you'll find them here, in order . . . or almost!

THE MYTH OF TOTAL SILENCE

Perhaps counter-intuitively, the first thing was to reconcile myself with my chattiness, to accept it as a normal fact of existence, and to become aware of the different factors contributing to the racket going on inside my head.

As an aside: have you ever noticed that the path of progression often seems to involve back-pedalling? That 'moving forward' is very often synonymous with 'going back to the source'? Evolving not through developing new qualities – absolute silence – but through starting off by accepting a few little imperfections. End of the aside, which was brought to you in a whisper, naturally.

So the rose-lined path we shall follow will be to give up on the idea of absolute and permanent silence . . . and by accepting this premise find ways to simply help create pockets of silence in our day-to-day lives.

The little voice in our heads

So let's begin with an important fact regarding our current subject. Totally silencing our words is almost impossible. Of course, we can stop talking for many hours, or even days: this is what we experience during meditation retreats, and numerous spiritual traditions promote silence as a practice in its own right (as we'll be seeing later on). But when our words do not pass our lips, they still continue to parade inside our heads, in neat rows like good little soldiers. Because unless the EEG is flat (a horizontal line on the machine, which is a fairly bad sign), our brains continue to function and therefore generate ideas, thoughts, reflections and so on.

This means that many people have a sort of constant 'little voice' in their heads, commenting, analysing, grumbling or even singing, depending on the situation. It's nothing to worry about, and this little voice, commonly known as our 'internal dialogue', is sometimes very useful. It was what gave me the inspiration to write this book, and string these sentences together, for example. It's the same little voice that provides your sparkling conversation at the office party, gives you food for thought on the subject of organic farming and vegetarianism, or dictates your shopping list. It's also the voice that says, with the resignation of someone fighting a losing battle, 'Hmmm, are you sure? You're not going to make that mistake again, are you?' when you swoon at the sight of a beautiful pair of eyes belonging to an Adonis, who happens to be married with three kids. And it will also be the one to come back with the classic, 'I told you so!' at the end of your colourful, but oh-so-brief adventure . . . but anyway . . .

Most of the time, the little voice chatters away inside us in an entirely ordinary way. Now of course, if the voice appears in the middle of the night telling you, 'I, Satan, command you to pick up this axe and go and scalp your neighbour!' it's probably time to go and see a 'mind doctor' (= psychiatrist) right away!

But in general, people talk to themselves inside their heads. And everyone finds it normal. Some people – not you, of course not! – even talk to themselves out loud in the car, at home, while they're doing the housework or tidying up the garage: 'Ah, there it is . . . Right, well I think I'm going to put it over there . . . OK . . . Good . . .' Sound familiar?

Language and perception

But the influence of words on our daily lives runs even deeper. In the late 20th century, numerous sociological studies showed that people's image of the world changes according to their culture and above all their language. Edward T. Hall discusses this beautifully in the introduction to his book *The Hidden Dimension*, which also explores the differences in personal space boundaries according to the country of origin: a mine of information to help us better understand people from different cultures.

Words change our perception and relationship to the world. The Inuit, for example, have fifty-two different words for snow, and their eyes have learnt to analyse the type of surface surrounding them in an instant. Hard snow, soft snow, thick snow, icy snow, aerated snow, compact snow . . . The precision of the term used is crucial and – although I don't claim any particular knowledge of Inuit life – can probably affect the group's survival. With this large palette of words available, they have become used to describing the snow around them more precisely. Children learn this from the earliest age, and so words help to sharpen their perception and knowledge of the world, or even to shape it. (Did words create thoughts or vice versa? Or did they both emerge together? A good subject for any budding student of philosophy!)

So we can see how deeply language impregnates our daily lives and our way of 'seeing the world'. An extremely interesting insight that maybe suggests we should question our habitual ways of seeing things more often, and to try out some new ones. An acquaintance of mine called G., who works as a therapist, regularly allows himself to change 'persona'. Some weekends, he dresses in a new style, invents a personal history, changes the rhythm of his sentences and his walk, and starts using new words. One day he might be a sportsman, another day a company boss, and another day a taxi driver . . . According to his enthusiastic reports, the world, and his perceptions of it, change completely. The character gains substance over the course of the day, and G. is fascinated by the new emotions he discovers. In this instance, language and lexical field play a very particular role. He says language is THE crucial detail that allows him to really enter into the experience. When he has found the right 'way of talking', the character becomes fluid and human connections are formed unexpectedly. Words and language have altered his perception of himself and others. How about that for opening up new possibilities?

But what does this have to do with silence? Simple. Since early childhood, we've learnt to name the things we come across. This is a table, this is a clock, an hour lasts sixty minutes, etc. This habit, which is extremely useful, incidentally, allows us to communicate and make ourselves understood. It also gives reassuring structure to our lives: by naming, we prove the existence of a given object and set boundaries on our environment. But this approach based on naming, this habit of defining and having an opinion, also has the effect of attaching preconceptions to things, to ourselves and to those around us. By defining our neighbour as a grouch, we put a label on her that closes off possibilities. So rediscovering silence could work something like this: looking at our neighbour through the curious, captivated eyes of a child, without prejudice or criticism in advance. She's just a human being, someone I discover or rediscover each day. I allow her the possibility, for one day, of no longer moaning – why not?

The joy of 'not knowing'

To sum up, we could say – at the risk of stating the obvious – that language = labels. A logical idea and no bad thing, because that's what words are for (and also for elegantly combining into poetry). Yet a problem quickly emerges, because by applying a label to something new, on the one hand we fill it up, but on the other hand we limit it. Silencing our words and concepts, or returning to a terminological 'void', offers us the incredible luxury of giving the world back its possibilities and freedom.

The idea here is to explore the joy of 'not knowing'. Because freeing ourselves from concepts is about remaining in the space before words, the inherently inexpressible space where unicorns are born. Hiking off to find the elusive treasure at the end of the rainbow. Daring to set off on an adventure with nothing in our pockets. And realising after coming back across the threshold that everything was already completely peaceful and silent, and always had been.

LEARNING TO BE QUIET

*Words that are not said are the flowers
of silence.*

Japanese proverb

Why it's so difficult

You've read the title of this section and I'll let you prepare
yourselves psychologically for the profound upheavals that
will be required. This is the price for access to calm and
silence. But do not fear, the result is equal to the 'sacrifice'.
Because for some of us, it really is a sacrifice, like cutting
off a part of ourselves, the part that constantly talks to
colleagues, neighbours or friends about the smallest details
of our lives . . . or the weather!

And Zen monasteries are no exception. Although they're
designed as spaces devoted to silence and meditation,
they're inhabited by people like you and me. Some residents
have a natural taste for silence, some have gradually
acquired it, and for others still it remains a form of torture.
Each morning, before meditation, we have twenty minutes
to have a wash before having a cup of tea in the communal
room. The rule of silence has been in force since the
previous evening. But a few people really struggle to be
in the company of others and drink a cup of tea without
exchanging complicit glances or little morning greetings.

As this is 'forbidden' to a greater or lesser extent, they do so furtively, in a whisper. For a long time, I wondered how it could be that complete silence was impossible? Why did we have this absolute compulsion for contact with others?

Talking to other people often actually seems to be an exercise in reassurance: I look at the other person and say hello, he or she returns the greeting with a few words, thus confirming my existence. Or, to put it another way, I exist through the other person's eye contact and words. Does this mean that otherwise I don't exist? It would take more than a whole book to explore this subject alone! Who am I? What is reality? Do I need social contact to survive? Philosophers and film-makers (think of *The Matrix*) have been only too happy to sow confusion and introduce little hints of uncertainty into our nicely ordered lives. The same goes for Buddhism, but I'll keep quiet on that – it's not for me to comment on . . .

Not speaking is cruelly at odds with our need to be seen, and heard. And this is why some people, who are probably more sensitive to other people's attention, find themselves ill at ease when they have to remain silent.

The benefits of keeping quiet

CALMING THE MIND

In Buddhism, this practice is known as 'Noble Silence'. It consists of keeping quiet and allowing the words that arise

THE GIFT OF SILENCE

to pass by, leaving them unspoken. Deciding, consciously and deliberately, not to talk. The benefits are numerous. And after a few hours, or a few days, the mind becomes calm.

Once a year, we hold a week's silent retreat, in mid-winter. In addition to the fairy-tale scenery with all the snow, this is a special time in which to really immerse ourselves in silence. The retreat, which is essentially given over to meditation, is called *rōhatsu*. It celebrates the Buddha's awakening 2,600 years ago, on 8 December (date to be confirmed, there were no selfies taken that day . . .). A week without talking: perfect conditions! Each year (this is my twelfth *rōhatsu*), I notice with renewed amazement the incredible effect of this silence on my mental activity. After a few hours, complete calm takes hold. There is even a sense of total contentment at the prospect of several days spent in nurturing calm.

In general, we have ideas, desires and remarks to make on everyday subjects: work, public transport, politics, etc. But if we 'forget' to formulate them, these subjects fairly quickly lose their importance. A dispute with a colleague that is not verbalised, and above all not discussed with our entire professional network, will end up unravelling like an old pullover, losing its original shape and significance altogether. It all depends on the dispute in question, of course – this isn't an absolute rule – but silence will certainly provide some space for the problem to be resolved. This is borne out by the common habit of going for a run in order to 'take your mind off things'. Jogging in silence – not enough breath to talk! – frees the mind from its internal rumbling. To the rhythm of your strides, the words gradually disappear, each leg like a painter's brush gently revealing the horizon. According to the wisest among us, the horizon – calm – is always there, beyond outward appearance. It doesn't take much for us to rediscover it.

Of course, in pragmatic terms, it's not always possible to free up a week for a silent meditation retreat. Especially the first time – because once people have experienced the joys of a new way of being, they often await the next spiritual appointment with impatience and plan their holidays accordingly. But if your diary is resolutely overbooked, you'll find a few ideas below to help you experiment with silence in your everyday life, without having to wait.

A DIFFERENT LANGUAGE

A few years ago, in 2008, I visited Japan for a traditional retreat (see Chapter 3). The nuns who taught at the monastery were quite traditionalist and some of them struggled to see how Zen Buddhism could have anything to do with 'foreigners', and involve other people besides the Japanese themselves. When I arrived, I was informed that English was forbidden and that everything would be conducted in the local language, Japanese. As is often the case in Japan, messages have 'secret drawers': there is what is said and what is not said; appearance and reality. In this case, the Abbess and one of her marvellous assistants had arranged things so that my dormitory contained all the nuns who spoke or could stumble through a few words of English. So there was the official message, 'It is forbidden to speak English', and the underlying sensitive approach, 'We will do everything we can so that you can still integrate.' It's a subtle and very interesting culture that I still love to explore.

But why this little story? During the three months of the retreat, I ended up having barely any verbal contact with the nuns. The instructions were in Japanese, with little translation for my benefit. Just enough to be able to follow without getting too lost. Most of the time, they talked animatedly amongst themselves, and I couldn't grasp the content of the conversation at all. In the beginning, with no language method, I tried to recognise sentence structures or intonation, but it was no good: Japanese was all Greek to me! So before very long at all, I stopped listening. Their nattering was like a familiar buzz that helped the days pass by and lent them a cheerful spontaneity: the nuns chattered a lot, creating a refreshing atmosphere with their shrieks and laughter. And I didn't understand a word of it!

The benefits were enormous. All my usual little complaints, by losing their preferred outlet, evaporated like snow in the sunshine. Enforced silence burnt off at the root any inclination to anger or resentment. There was no one to moan or grumble with, no audience to whom I could express my opinion on anything or everything: these were certainly the ideal conditions in which to develop a new way of thinking, by inviting in silence. To tell you the truth my little inner soundtrack continued but . . . in Japanese! Having become used to my internal dialogue over so many years, it was impossible to silence it, or at least I didn't even envisage the possibility. I needed something, a little reassuring internal noise. And so a new language appeared: little phrases in Japanese, Buddhist chants and sutras . . . An everyday mental soundtrack beyond all logical sense. I was very fond of it. And each day, I felt more peaceful and focused.

You don't need to travel to the other side of the world to experience this; a simple moment of consciousness, a detachment from your interior dialogue, is all that is needed. The words that parade through our heads have a life of their own and, strange though it might seem, it's possible to hear them as if they were the voice of someone else, and so to detach from them completely. Learning to get to know our inner voice better means we can learn to forget about it from time to time in order to reconnect with the present moment.

For me, the unfamiliar, new language I was surrounded by forced me to become a student of my own mind, studying the little voice inside my head as a scientist might observe a cell under the microscope, amazed to hear it speaking Japanese just to fill the space. In observing this unexpected voice, I managed to detach myself from it; words lost their hypnotic power over me. And from this comes a great sense of freedom.

Including the fact that I have an inner dialogue inside my head that is hell-bent on expressing itself, whatever the circumstances! And even capable of speaking Japanese just to fill the space! The appearance of this new language was so unexpected that I began to observe it carefully, and above all to detach myself from it. You could say that the words had lost their hypnotic power. The little voice inside my head became a subject of study, like a scientist might observe a cell under the microscope. I became a student of my own mind and, thanks to this form of witness-presence, gained a profound sense of freedom in return!

HEARING MORE, OPENING THE DOORS OF PERCEPTION

If the doors of perception were cleansed,
everything would appear to man as it is, Infinite.

William Blake

When our little inner voice speaks up, there is a sound. Loud or soft, high, medium or low. The sound is generally notice-able enough to cut us off from the sonic world surrounding us. To put it another way, we cannot 'chatter in our heads' and hear the sounds of the world at the same time. More's the pity! As a result, so many people will go for a walk in the forest with friends without even noticing the melody of the trees, the little gasp of an autumn leaf coming off a branch, the creaking of bark . . . But out of the blue, as if by surprise, the mouth falls silent and the head with it. Suddenly, we can hear again! We walk with our steps hammering on the ground and the sound penetrates the moment. This sensation of 'presence' is experienced when we feel everything is there, in place, and the 'I' can disappear into the wider world. We sometimes feel it when we stand at the top of a mountain, or contemplate the ocean. It can be fleeting and quickly forgotten, but other times it will make a profound impression on the person who experiences it.

Are you familiar with the impression of immensity that can suddenly appear during a walk? A sort of vertigo in response to the scale of it all, the imprint of a heart that suddenly beats faster, perhaps as it falls into step with the rhythm of the universe. Some describe it as a feeling that 'we are not alone', others fall to their knees to pray to God, and still others accept the mystery as it is, without raising the veil, allowing the adventure of the unknown into their lives.

But whether in the city or in the countryside, people who choose to stay quiet, to resist the urge to talk, perceive a different world: a sense of suspension, a pause, an unfurled energy. Was it always there or did it appear thanks to our observation? Hard to tell, but it is as if the sounds, the nearest to the most distant, have opened up to our ears.

Amongst practitioners of Buddhism, one of the favourite figures is Kannon, also known as Avalokiteshvara or Chenrezi: the Buddha of Compassion. She is often represented as a goddess, with a thousand arms, or thereabouts. Certain traditions use this image or archetype to find inspiration in daily life. By imagining all of this Buddha's qualities, you encourage the mind to move towards them. Kannon's other name is

'She who hears the sounds of the world', and I often like to talk about her when welcoming newcomers. Her message is one of extraordinary warmth. Kannon hears everything, knows all of the world's inhabitants – their lives, their qualities, their defects, their desires – and observes all this with the most infinite compassion. After having heard so many things over so many years, the only emotion she is left with is a benevolent affection for human nature.

Perhaps her example could simply encourage us to make friends with ourselves? (The sentiment expressed in a splendid book by the Tibetan nun Pema Chödrön*, a highly recommended read.)

EXERCISES FOR CLEARING THE MIND
AND SILENCING THE INNER CRITIC

The experience of sound travel

To earn my living, I have various, equally fascinating jobs, including my work as a singing teacher. People come for individual lessons or on courses, in the centre of Strasbourg, to discover the basics of vocal functioning, breathing and resonance. Most of the time, students squeeze their classes into the middle of the day, between two other activities, and burst in for the sessions full of their urban buzz. They arrive wrapped up in their preoccupations, ready for anything apart

....

* *The Wisdom of No Escape: How to Love Yourself and Your World*, 2004

from concentrating and feeling! So I've introduced a helpful little ritual: the decompression chamber. It's quite simple to do, at any point in the day, sitting, standing, lying down, alone or in the middle of a crowd. Plus, it's invisible and undetectable! So you can do it anywhere – at a meeting, on the train, at home with your family – without being noticed, which wouldn't be the case with a traditional meditation session or breathing exercise.

THE DECOMPRESSION CHAMBER

So this is the exercise: wherever you are at the moment, become aware of the sounds all around you. Listen to sounds close by, then those in the distance. Take the time to move from one space to another, from the foreground to the background. Then listen out for the different frequencies: high, low, medium. Try to distinguish all the sounds at that point in time: the dull throb of the city, the trains passing in the distance, the squealing of brakes, the noise of the wind in the trees, a car wash, conversations . . . The secret lies in allowing the sounds to come to you and welcoming them in.

After a few minutes, a question might occur to you: where is the boundary between the inside and the outside? Where is the point where the sound is outside my ears, then moves into them? It's tricky, and subtle, but it's as if the boundary dissolves. Neither inside nor outside. Sounds, the world and the 'self' intimately intermingled. And opening up our sound field really does produce such a sense of well-being. The results are clear to see, as all my pupils agree unanimously: it's amazing how good you feel after five minutes of sound travelling: your breathing settles, your body becomes more present and a sensation of calm appears.

But why does this make us feel so good? Well, this is my theory: when we're worried, when we're turning our thoughts over in our minds and dwelling on them, we're functioning in a loop, in a closed circuit, like prisoners inside ourselves. We can walk down the whole length of a street without seeing it, absorbed in our inner monologue. By deciding to open the hatches and open our ears, space itself opens up in response. The 'external' world reappears, the monologue calms down, and our energies are restored to harmony as a result. Similarly, in therapy, the first task with someone suffering episodes of depression is to get them to look up and rediscover the landscape that surrounds them. In the practice described above, we do this by opening our ears: the result is identical, and the mood is considerably lightened as a result.

Taming the little voice inside you

As we mentioned earlier, real chatterboxes often have a sort of alias inside their heads, a sort of Jiminy Cricket or Tinkerbell talking (or tinkling) ten to the dozen from morning to night. Officially, this is known as our 'internal dialogue', but 'monologue' would probably be more appropriate, because unless you answer yourself out loud (which is a bit of a risk if you want to keep a normal social life), the little voice is generally talking all on its own.

I can offer you three practices to help you to moderate the audio stream from this little voice. A whole book could be written just on the subject of its origin, usefulness and credibility, because once again we're touching on the mystery of consciousness. But instead, let's study the little voice from a practical perspective, in order to regain a measure of calm and inner silence.

THE ROYAL APPROACH:
OBSERVING WITHOUT TOUCHING

We could also call this the 'Path of Kings'. It's the practice that stands firm when all others have been tested. The one that takes us furthest and offers the

---

most possibilities. It's my favourite – by a long way – so I've chosen to introduce you to it first. It might not look like much, but appearances can be deceptive, and this is no exception.

First of all, sit down somewhere calm. Close your eyes or keep them half closed, but very, very relaxed. Then stand up, adopt the royal pose of someone about to do something important, or even sacred. It's time to set off on an exploration of your thoughts. What are you thinking about? But most importantly, what words are currently being spoken? Are they logical discourses or snatches of phrases, or even a song you've just heard? Is it your voice that is speaking, or the voice of a friend, or does it belong to one of your parents?

Now we are at the heart of the exercise, what it all comes down to: it doesn't take much to gradually calm this little voice and free up periods of silence. Simply adopt the position of a neutral observer. This is also known as witness consciousness, the faculty of observing the thoughts and words that appear without acting, judging or commenting. In this state of observation, we are simultaneously associated with the experience and disconnected from it, inside and outside. Just being there and allowing them to pass by, whilst remaining fully aware of every little word.

THE SECRET

To achieve this neutral observer position, stand upright in a very straight posture, above all absolutely still, with your eyes calmly directed towards the ground, half open to let just a few fragments of light through. It is this immobility that makes the body available and ready; this very powerful posture combines the power of a samurai with a deep gentleness. Often our minds, in a sort of wild dance, will fill the spaces with thoughts, opinions and desires, all in a closed circuit. In letting all of these circulate and then disappear, a new space full of calm – a new breathing space if you like – can appear.

This practice has the advantage of offering a genuine 'reconciliation' with ourselves. We're not going to fight the voice, try to create some empty space, or offer it any suggestions for improvements. Like The Doors song, we're just going to 'take it as it comes'. From a psychological point of view, the idea is for everyone to accept themselves as they are, with their qualities, their defects and their inner voices that are sometimes brilliant, sometimes dictatorial and sometimes critical, all the aspects of ourselves accepted with the same tranquillity. They are simply held up in front of the mirror of our witness consciousness. At this point, left untouched, the thought/voice appears and then disappears naturally. The result is an incredible sensation of freedom! And we can develop a new relationship to ourselves and to the world, which is simultaneously more serene and more tolerant.

PLAYING WITH OUR LITTLE VOICE

The little voice also provides an excellent opportunity to have a bit of fun and rediscover our childhood spirit. Some things will probably have you in fits of laughter, others will take you by surprise. But in any event, you will be amazed at your brain's abilities and the possibility of taking back a little control, which is available to everyone. So, if your little voice sometimes annoys you, follow the guide!

- **Find your little voice**: this step is the same as in the previous exercise. Initially, you'll find it much easier to do it somewhere calm, but with a little practice, you'll be able to do it on the train, walking around, while doing your shopping, etc.

- **Turn down the volume**: imagine a volume control or a cursor near your head. Start by making the voice louder by turning up the volume, then turn it down. The voice gets quieter: magic, isn't it?

- **Relocate**: where do you hear this voice? Is it in your head, above it, near your right ear, your left ear, at the back of your head, down near your throat? Take the time to find it and pin down its location, then . . . suggest it moves. The voice follows the movement. It changes location! Next, experiment with the perfect place, where it can leave you in peace when you need some calm. Personally, I often put it by my heart: that way, it retains its primary protective function (the little voice knows many, many things) but leaves my head free to observe the world.

You can find lots of other little exercises that all stem from NLP (neuro-linguistic programming). I often use them in therapy with very positive results. One young woman, for instance, had a dictatorial inner voice that sent out negative signals from morning to night: 'You're good for nothing . . . Ridiculous! . . . You'll never do it like that . . . You're just clumsy, you useless girl,' etc. We didn't look for the origins of all this, but instead worked directly on the content. I suggested she should replace her voice with Donald Duck's voice. Besides a session full of giggles and beneficial tears, it became impossible for her to take the criticism seriously. Donald's voice cancelled everything out, allowing a feeling of joyful freedom to emerge.

THE BODY AND THE VOICE (OR HOW TO 'PULL A DOPEY FACE')

Body and mind are closely linked. This idea also applies to one of the most amazing organs in the human body: the tongue. With its seventeen muscles, it can perform all kinds of movements. It's the reason we can speak brilliantly and eloquently, whether babbling to a baby or giving the speech of your life at the company's AGM. Thanks to your tongue, you can say 'I love you' or say goodbye to your grandmother just before her final journey . . . So it's a very useful organ but often also ultra-tense!

Relaxing the tongue has the immediate effect of slowing down the flow of words in our minds. It would seem – even if there have been no studies on the subject yet – that the tongue is intimately linked to our internal dialogue. So relaxing one appears to calm the other. I've very often experienced this in meditation, to my great delight.

THE DOPEY FACE EXERCISE

But how do we relax the tongue? In fact, you need to relax the tongue and jaw *together*. Let your jaw drop, even if you have to partly open your mouth and allow the tongue to rest behind the teeth. You'll appreciate that the resulting expression doesn't convey a great degree of intelligence. But that's the price for relaxation! The exercise is also known as 'Droopy-the-dog face'. Try it out (in private) and you will notice that the relaxation purely and simply stops you from moaning, dwelling on something or grumbling inside your head. As a friend recently said to me, 'Imagine if just pulling a dopey face was the miracle solution to all our problems!' . . . I'll let you be the judge.

$$\left(5 \right)$$

Bodily silence

Fifteen years ago, if someone had described my current life to me, I would probably have been knocked for six. So would this life have appealed to me from my perspective back then? All those hours spent in the silence of nature, observing the changing skies, unlocking the mysteries of animals and observing all the resonances and rhythms of my body with the greatest attention. In fact, back then I didn't really think about my body. At the most it was an object that I lugged willingly or otherwise from party to party and from one extreme experience or adventure to the next, in order to pass the time. But singing and meditation changed everything. A new world appeared, as I gradually became more present in my body, organ by organ, until I slowly regained every sensation, or almost.

But it took time, and a lot of patience. I remember my first experience of meditation at the Zen temple of La Gendronnière in central France. Sitting cross-legged on the cushion, the master showed us all the different parts of the body to observe in order to adopt an erect posture: legs, spine, nape of the neck, top of the head and even . . . the contact between our thumbs. The idea was to press the thumbs together delicately, as if we were holding a little ant: not too hard (you can imagine the result), nor too lightly (the little ant makes a run for it, incidentally never having been asked its opinion on taking part in the meditation in the first place . . .). Personally, my ant quickly met its maker the first few times, and hundreds of other ants summoned up for the exercise soon met the same fate: either escaping or being sacrificed on the altar of concentration. Luckily they were virtual ants!

As you'll have realised, my body awareness left something to be desired. But it developed, gradually, thanks to various little exercises that you'll find over the next few pages. But first, let's turn our attention to the following questions. Why the body? What are the benefits of body awareness? And after we've seen how important it is, the concept of 'bodily silence' will reveal its wonders . . . and its promises.

ARE WE TOO FAR REMOVED FROM OUR BODIES?

Come with me . . . I'd like to invite you first of all into the intimate environment of a singing lesson. After all, the body is essential if you want to sing. And this example will help us to realise, if need be, the crucial importance of rethinking our relationship to the body.

The secrets of a singing lesson

'Hello, are you Kankyo?' A young woman is standing in front of me, looking at me shyly, with a lock of hair over one eye. 'That's me, come on in . . .' At the first singing lesson, there's always something fascinating and magical about this first contact. We're about to set off on tip-toe to discover each other's worlds. We're going to navigate the mystery of our characters, with absolute honesty. We're going to laugh, confide in each other, and share this simply offered gift: the wonder of our voices, breath and bodies resonating in the most natural way in the world, thanks to their sound, without thinking for a moment about the miracle that made it possible.

'Would you like something to drink? Coffee, green tea? We're going to have a bit of a chat first, before we move on to the serious stuff!'

'Oh, a cup of coffee would be lovely . . .' says the young woman quietly, with an embarrassed smile.

I leave her for a few moments while I make the coffee. A little silence, just enough for her to hear the beating of her heart. A silence that is broken well before the contours of the room come into sharp focus.

'So, tell me, why do you want to take singing lessons?' I ask, sitting down next to her.

'Oh, it's for my boyfriend,' she immediately replies. 'He's in an electro band and I do the backing singing. But I can see that I lack technique . . . I'd like my voice to be a bit

113

more confident . . . Apart from that, I like the blues and French singers like Camille or Christine and the Queens.'

Her smile is hesitant but also gutsy. She's tall, but stoops, with her head tucked into her shoulders, like a child being told off. Maximum protection.

'Do you do any sport?'

'Yes, I swim lengths of the pool. It's quite boring, but you know . . .' she says, as if apologising for something.

'Well, with the teaching methods I use, there's a very bodily aspect to singing. Most of our work will be to do with the body. So, with people like you who do some sport, who are used to moving, it's much easier. You'll see . . . So shall we make a start?'

We go over to the teaching room, which is at the other end of the place I rent for my lessons. It's a huge space, all white and calm, designed for the practice of Zen Buddhism: a Zen Centre, where traditional meditation takes place morning and evening, with chanting of sutras and incense offerings. But during the day, with some rare exceptions, the place remains empty, so I'm lucky enough to have a peaceful atmosphere to work in, just occasionally broken by the noise of the car wash outside. With a little imagination, the hissing of the water pumps could resemble waves breaking on the ocean . . . and serenity is preserved!

We go past the meditation room with its light wood and black cushions scattered around, and open the door of the activity room: around sixty square metres, five-metre ceilings and a beige carpet on the floor.

'This is my room. But it's a secret! Whatever you do, don't tell anyone there's a place like this right in the middle of town, they'd want to steal it!' I joke.

'It's a really nice, really relaxing space,' says the young woman, whose name is Aurélie.

'You can leave your shoes here. We're going to get comfortable . . . The first lesson always starts with some work on regaining awareness of the body, on physical sensation. So we're going to . . . explore! And to begin with, the first thing is to say hello to our bodies, to regain that awareness of them, to do what Zen masters call 'going home'. In our western societies, we have very highly developed brains. Probably a little too developed! Unfortunately, the price for this development is paid by our bodies. Today, we're going to get back in contact with our musical instrument, tune it up and allow it to resonate. It will do it good to feel like someone's paying it some attention! So stand up, spread your arms like a bird and enjoy: take advantage of this feeling of space and freedom . . .'

Aurélie dutifully closed her eyes, brows furrowed, still wondering what the rest of the lesson might have in store, given the surprise of the introduction. But curiosity got the better of her and soon she spread her arms wide above her head. And together, we delighted in this incredible sensation of the body expanding its boundaries.

For many people, this moment is the start of a long process of re-enchantment with the body. All those years at school spent cultivating our critical senses, learning things like the periodic table, have orphaned us from an important part of ourselves. Those endless hours memorising the dates of the kings and queens (which we forget just as quickly) have left our bodies as prisoners of the rational, languishing like the Count of Monte Cristo in the shade of the mind, forgotten beneath the vestiges of thought with a capital T.

Obviously, lots of us did sport at school or played tennis or football outside school. But often, the magic of physical *culture* was lacking. It was about performance, pushing limits, techniques, notes on the bulletin board and everything that ultimately gets in the way of the close communion between mind and body. Although I performed gymnastics at a high level for nearly ten years, I have no memory of having heard a single word celebrating the beauty of move-ment. On the contrary, it was all about getting your recalcitrant body to bend, keeping it on a tight leash, and ignorantly forcing it to become the instrument of your own glory. All to win medals and convince yourself that you're finally worth something.

The gulf between this conception and Taoist thinking, in which the body is a temple to contain primordial energy, and in which purification rituals celebrate the sacred nature of incarnation, is . . . as vast as the Great Wall of China!

A balloon on a string: sad but true

But that's not all. Rudolf Steiner, the famous educationalist and creator of the schools of the same name, came up with quite a striking image of our modern disharmony. He liked to compare twentieth-century children to balloons, with a big balloon (the head) and a little string (the body and everything 'below the head'). The main thrust of this image was to criticise an educational system that placed all the emphasis on intelligence, in the intellectual sense of the term, whilst ignoring the rest. So what is the rest? Merely our organs, sensations, emotions, fluids, energy flows . . . a whole forgotten world! This disdain for the body – probably the result of Catholicism and its vilification of anything closely or distantly related to pleasure – has spawned generations of empty shells impaired in their ability to feel, 'eggheads' with no connection to the Earth.

These days, in spite of a general awareness of this imbalance, the situation still appears quite worrying in certain respects: millions of teenagers are effectively born with mobile phones attached to their hands, like an extension of their bodies. They may have gained another organ, but the real issue is that they have become prisoners of a new tool for escape into the virtual world. When it comes to setting up and intuitively using their devices, they're highly skilled! But when it comes to living their lives mindfully, controlling the stimuli they receive and deciding whether to respond, the battle seems to have been lost: a text arrives, the smartphone owner's hand whips out and grabs it. No conscious choice: the sequence plays out automatically, without any sensation of 'presence' (see page 99). TV and internet play the same role, generating long periods of absence, like organised trances. Need some proof? How about this example: we're engrossed in a film, the hero opens a refreshing can of drink, and when the adverts come on, there we are, opening the fridge like robots.

The virtual world, with its promotion of make-believe, overshadows the possibility of a life lived in the flesh, to the full, with its tragedies and its splendours. The way we present our lives on social media, creating an imaginary reality, offers very little space for the natural development of a human being: gradually learning to accept our limits, develop our potential and reconcile ourselves with our bodies as they are, rather than as we imagine them.

So now we can take Rudolf Steiner's image of the balloon, with the big head/little body, and imagine the balloon is inflated with helium, a gas characterised by its extreme lightness, like these virtual, superficial, imaginary worlds . . . taking us ever further from the Earth.

Why are we so disconnected from our bodies?

So why, then? Why is it so difficult to 'return to the body'? Because the body is so closely bound to reality. In entirely pragmatic terms, the body breathes, digests, resonates and feels emotions (fear, joy, disgust, desire, etc.). If we pay attention, we realise that these emotions are experienced inside the body. Numerous popular expressions bear this out, phrases like, 'I have a knot in my stomach' or, 'I can feel it in my guts' or even, 'love is blind' (the idea that passion is pretty much divorced from reason . . . a whole new subject in itself!).

So our bodies and our emotions are closely linked. Cutting ourselves off from our bodies means we can scrupulously avoid any negative emotion and remain purely on the surface of things . . . until the body catches up with us one day, with one of its trademark psychosomatic complaints. It's very often a prolonged situation of stress, an unexpressed sadness or a daily sense of discontentment that leads to the emergence of chronic high blood pressure, a stomach ulcer or recurrent eczema. All these are signs of emotions that have been ignored and are looking for a means of expression at all costs. And the outlet they find is the body, which, far from staying silent, uses all of its intuitive intelligence to send us a message. In its own way, in an effort to make us do something, it stamps its feet, reacts and shouts. It's as if the body moves away from its natural state of silence, its original harmony, in order to send the brain an urgent request for change.

But very often, human beings lack the tools to process this sort of request. We didn't learn how to manage our emotions at school, we don't know how our thoughts work, we're afraid of being submerged and prefer to cut ourselves off from sensations with the help of all the distractions that modern society offers. This is the realm of bulimia, addictions and other palliatives that allow us to cut ourselves off from our overflowing emotions. The body is forgotten, as a survival reflex, because we know no other way of reacting. This is also what happens naturally when we suffer a trauma. Victims of war, rape or serious accidents dissociate themselves from the suffering body, which is the only way to survive. Or approaching from the opposite direction, those who treat them often try to create this dissociation from pain – by encouraging a patient to take refuge in a happy memory – so that they can perform emergency surgery, for example. This method is reserved for serious traumas, however, and unless that's your description of life, then being fully present in your body holds many advantages.

This is why sages have worked for millennia to supply us with methods to reconnect with our bodies and learn to manage our negative emotions. And here they are.

A NEW RELATIONSHIP WITH THE BODY: LEARNING TO FEEL

The Path of Freedom

All branches of spirituality and philosophy unanimously agree that the Path of Freedom involves learning to feel. What could be better than becoming completely free of our emotions, to know them well enough to be able to rediscover a quality of existence? Because by cutting ourselves off from our bodies (through habit or because we have not learnt to do otherwise), we also cut ourselves off from pleasures like these: feeling refreshing summer rain on our foreheads, jumping for joy and discovering that this energy really brings the whole body to life, eating a meal that brings tears of pleasure to our eyes, feeling the scent of the earth and its humus penetrate our cells, stretching out on the grass like a cat then crawling on all fours with our noses to the ground to breath in the fragrances of the meadow . . .

So the body gives us access to pleasure. I'll discreetly leave you to imagine all the implications of that statement. But it goes even further than that: it could rightly be said that presence in the body is the only way to tie us closely into the present moment.

The present instant = the body. Full stop. Living in the here and now entails being able to feel your body, in real time. So extracting ourselves from our bodies would implicitly mean agreeing to live elsewhere, in the virtual sphere, all alone in our idealised worlds.

Emotions are sensations

For years, different schools of psychology disagreed on this point. One side believed that emotions originated in the brain: you think about a friend who has passed away, then feel the sadness in your body. The other side proposed the opposite origin: an unpleasant feeling in the solar plexus, that your brain quickly analyses to discover the cause. But now the issue has resolved itself harmoniously: both schools were right. Sometimes it's one, sometimes the other. Aside from the emergence of a Middle Way, which would always find favour with me, these two possibilities are united by the important role played by the body. Whatever happens, there will be an effect on the body, conscious or otherwise. And therefore, as we'll see later, the possibility of changing things.

When it comes to our representation of the world, or 'what's inside our heads', we've seen that we think in the form of images, our 'little voice' or bodily sensations (see Chapters 3 and 4). And this last category is the one we're interested in here. It's also known as our kinaesthetic sense. To experience it for yourself, shut your eyes for a moment (after you've read the next few lines) and concentrate on your body (you know, the big thing underneath your head). Feel the different parts of your body, at random. Feel whether it's hot or cold. Feel its rhythms, circulation, heaviness, lightness, etc. Do you have a particular emotion in your body? If so, where is it situated? Take a bit of time, and a whole world opens up to you. If you're dealing with a fairly unpleasant emotion, be sure to stop the exercise quickly. If it's a very pleasant emotion, take advantage and then . . . share!

You've just discovered one of the forms that our thoughts can take. Certain people have a preference for this channel and feel a lot through their bodies. They generally like to wear soft clothes and cannot conceive of any human relationship without physical contact. For a kinaesthetic person, the absence of hand or other body contact is a form of rejection that will make them quite uneasy. So in our visually dominated (contactless) western society, the life of a kinaesthetic person is full of little bumps in the road that upset them without them knowing why. They are blessed with an abundance of feelings – an expanded world of sensations – but at the same time distressed at not knowing what to do with it.

What to do with our emotions?

There are different approaches open to us: some are concrete and pragmatic, others more spiritual. In either case, by practising these exercises we can rediscover a more relaxed relationship with our bodies, with a different rhythm in which silence and calm play an integral part.

THE SPIRITUAL METHOD: UNLIMITED ACCEPTANCE

As you might suspect, this is my preferred method. It goes well beyond mere personal development and could even – according to the enlightened – put us on first name terms with the angels. It's tempting to believe, particularly since in Buddhism, we ourselves are the angels!

Half-angel, half-demon, the less charitable might reply. But no! Real angels, made of flesh and blood. The spiritual method proposes nothing short of (re)discovering our 'Original Nature', which is traditionally known as the 'Buddha Nature'. Everyone has one; everyone is a Buddha in the making, an angel, a miraculous being . . . but this splendour is very often hidden behind the opaque shrouds of our rational thought.

123

The spiritual method encourages us to adopt a new paradigm: to infuse our lives with a revelatory product that allows the infinite to emerge. The images that emerge are truly radiant. The best possible version of 'ourselves' in the guise of luminescent angels. (Note to the reader: to those who might be concerned to see me talking to the angels, yes, I'm writing in my normal state, with a bit of a cold, I'll admit, but no drugs. It's just that the occasional experience of the soul of the world inspires such *enthusiasm*, a word that derives from the Greek for 'letting God in'. What? My explanation just makes things worse? In that case, I'll leave you in the hands of the angels . . . *Namaste* . . .)

But what is this revelatory, miraculous product that illuminates our days and allows our Buddha/angel nature to emerge? It is simply – and in alchemy, the simplest methods are often the most effective – the filter of unconditional love.

THE KNIGHT'S PATH:
ACCEPTING YOUR EMOTIONS

Here are the instructions: whatever emotion appears, allow it to exist and disappear without intervening. Note the emergence of the emotion, whatever it is, in one or more parts of your body, and allow it to vanish in a natural process. To make this possible, you need to have an inner attitude of unconditional love for your emotions. Every emotion that passes through us is accepted, without being judged, rejected or harboured. In general, methods give us a 'trick' for changing what we don't like and moving towards what we do. We try to get rid of fears, sadness and stress. This is logical and justified, of course, and is also the route we'll be pursuing in the following sections. But the spiritual method goes much further. It encourages us to sit down in the heart of the volcano and let our fears dissolve. It's called the knight's path because it requires courage and determination. But it is also the path of reconciliation, the end of hostilities and the acceptance of everything that is part of us, the 'good' as well as the 'bad' (these two adjectives are deliberately put in inverted commas because life often teaches us that things are not fixed . . .). The first step, essentially: an intuition that whispers to us, softly at first but then ever more loudly, 'You're great! It's wonderful! Everything is OK.'

But in more concrete terms, what are we talking about?

Sitting in silence, once again allow yourself to become aware of the emotions you feel in your body. Do not struggle; simply observe what is happening, thanks to an inner attitude of boundless acceptance. Observe everything, like a curious mirror, and allow everything to disappear as fast as it appeared. This is what we mean by unconditional love; the ability to accept everything that makes a human being, in its entirety.

THE BONUS GIFT

It's only after having felt this most tender feeling of love for yourself that you will be able to envelop others in your human warmth, with the utmost discretion, and spread joy around you.

THE SECRET

Should a powerful emotion emerge, observe it in brief snatches, for a few moments, and alternate with awareness of your abdominal breathing. If poorly practised, observation can sometimes increase the emotion rather than making it disappear. The problem here is that rather than truly observing, we are focusing 'from the inside', in a sense, and the dimension of vastness is missing: observing as if in a closed circuit within the body, without the peaceful connection to the space surrounding us.

A LITTLE FRIENDLY ADVICE

In Buddhism, we insist on the idea of practising in a group with a guide. This outside assistance gives us security and allows us to go out and confront our demons (or dragons, since we are being knights) with complete confidence.

THE SHAMANIC METHOD

A shaman forms the link between the Earth and material life and the world of the spirits, or Heaven. Using certain prayers or incantations, he reweaves the coloured brocade that links the two dimensions of our lives. In this exercise, the idea is for you to become the shaman of your own life: reconnect with your body, truly inhabit your incarnation in order to liberate your emotions and feel yourselves free. Quite a feat.

I discovered this magical technique during my hypnosis studies and immediately adopted it. It has the ability to calm numerous inner tensions or painful emotions and make room for something else.

THE WHEEL OF LIFE EXERCISE

Find a calm place where you won't be disturbed. Take the time to think about the pleasant emotion you would like to swap for your current emotion. To find it, you could think about one of the best times of your life, for example. What emotion were you feeling at that point? Whereabouts in the body did you feel it? Think back, and this simple evocation will allow you to rediscover the original sensation. This stage can take two minutes. Then connect yourself to your body and the negative emotion that sometimes appears and restricts your abilities. Where is it situated? What size is it within the body?

And now we come to the wheel of life: emotions are a movement, as the etymology of the word suggests (*e movere*: that which sets in motion). You're going to encourage this emotion in your body to start moving again and begin to move it slowly and deliberately in a circular motion. Then accelerate the movement – a little – and feel its hold increase . . . temporarily.

(Note: You have to fully feel the unpleasant emotion before you can allow it to disappear, in a few moments. But just through this action, by setting it in motion, we can already regain control over the sensation and allow the energy to circulate once more. The wheel of life – and this is its main advantage – allows us to escape from stagnation, extract ourselves from the emotional marshes to realise that when the mud settles at the bottom of the pond, the water on the surface becomes clear again.)

This is the moment; gradually slow down the circular movement that intensified the emotion and feel the effect of this progressive braking: its hold diminishes proportionally.

But we don't leave it at that, because nature abhors a vacuum. The wheel of life will allow us to replace the emotion/negative sensation with another, much more pleasant feeling. Here's how: now that the unpleasant emotion has disappeared or at least been calmed, activate the wheel of life *in the other direction*. And allow a positive sensation to emerge from the depths, expanding as it goes. Take advantage of this creation, feeling and participating in the process. If you now start turning the wheel even faster, the emotion itself will intensify until you are suffused with happiness, joy or well-being . . . tick the appropriate box.

Personally, I like to finish this exercise with a burst of laughter that releases lots of energy and leaves myriad joyful tremors in its wake.

THE BONUS GIFT

Besides ridding you of many of your negative emotions, this exercise, which should be practised regularly, allows you to reconnect to your body and develop great self-knowledge.

THE SECRET

The secret lies in alternating between two sharply differentiated emotions. So take plenty of time to activate your positive emotion, the wonderful memory you have in reserve. Visualise it in all its details and bathe in happiness before moving on to the wheel of life.

A LITTLE FRIENDLY ADVICE

I regularly include this exercise in hypnotherapy sessions. It allows us to grapple with numerous 'negative' emotional sensations to then invite them to dance. Start with little things that upset you on a daily basis before tackling stronger emotions. This way, you can begin by really mastering the method before gradually progressing.

DANCING, PINA BAUSCH STYLE

The wonderful choreographer Pina Bausch wanted to get everyone dancing: young, old, beautiful, ugly, yellow, black, white . . . Dance without borders. She created stunning spectacles in which humanity unfolded in all its rich diversity and fragility. With Pina Bausch, there are no starched tutus or little feet imprisoned in pointe shoes. Instead, the feet are free to move and the clothes are modern and silken. This is art at its peak, instilling the sacred into the everyday.

And this approach of instilling the sacred into the everyday might well be our calling. What could be more joyful than imagining our lives as works of art? Like choreographic performances to be invented step by step?

So now, I'm going to suggest a dance exercise that even the clumsiest amongst us can still fully embrace. Because even hippopotamuses can move with elegance (see Disney's *Fantasia*), so why not us? And since I recommend that you do the exercise in private, you can explore to your heart's content!

I discovered the technique on my NLP (neuro-linguistic programming) courses and was won over by its effectiveness, combined with its playful aspect. Since then, I've often used it in my sessions, not to mention prescribing it for myself when dealing with temporary emotional blockages.

DANCING EXERCISE

Choose a sensation/emotion connected to a current situation that is not particularly pleasant. Come up with a phrase to symbolise it. For example, 'I'm stuck', 'I'm on edge', 'I'm sad'. And start dancing while you repeat this phrase. Put a lot of space into your movements, spreading your arms wide, like a flock of wild geese in flight. Make your movements fluid, spinning and swaying as you repeat the phrase for two to three minutes. You could choose some generous, joyful music to help you: a bit of Mozart would go down nicely.

THE SECRET

The negative feeling is a stagnant emotion, which has become blocked. Restoring its impetus, setting it in motion, then changing its course (redirecting it) allows us to access other feelings and to set it free. And the body's fluidity becomes the reflection of inner fluidity.

THE EFFECT

After a few moments, you feel that the phrase and the emotion linked to it have lost their power. It's difficult, for example, to feel stuck when you're spreading your wings. It's difficult to be angry when you're making smooth, slow, undulating movements. There's a lack of congruence between the two attitudes, which makes room for change. And for a while, your brain will find it amusing to be 'on edge'.

A LITTLE FRIENDLY ADVICE

Anything goes when it comes to restoring some life to our poor, forgotten bodies. Dancing, running, rolling in the hay or walking in the rain. Anything to escape from our automatic thought production unit, aka 'the head'. Anything to reconnect with the magic of a breath of wind on our cheek or of our bare feet on the damp grass.

THE SILENT BODY

*Do not abandon movement to seek tranquillity,
look for tranquillity in movement.*

Taoist proverb

A tea ceremony

During a Zen retreat in Japan, I was lucky enough to receive
lessons in the tea ceremony according to the Urasenke
tradition. This is a true Spiritual Path impregnating every
aspect of daily life. For the lessons, we went to the tea
pavilion, which was surrounded by a splendid garden I
could have spent hours looking at . . . But mostly, contemplation wasn't the order of the day, and the nuns had to
engage in a string of activities from morning to night, as a
sign of good health, devotion and commitment to their
practice. The lessons were given by a little nun in her
seventies who came to the monastery two or three times a
week. At the end of the lessons, after a ceremony lasting
three hours, our legs were aching: prolonged periods in
seiza (kneeling on the tatami) took their toll on even the
toughest of us. But that wasn't the important part. The tea
ceremony has been handed down over centuries and follows
precise movements in a timeless ritual with an attention to
detail that is absent from most of what we learn in the
modern world. So this was our invitation to dive back into

the past, delivered with extreme politeness and precision as sharp as a samurai sword.

The gift that I took away from these sessions was about the importance of movements, their control and their elegance. To enter the room, to greet others or to clean out your tea bowl, you are taught a set body movement. Neither too much, nor too little. You simply perform the silent movement. I loved turning the bowl over in my hands, feeling the smooth contours of these age-old wooden objects, observing the fluidity of the tea master's movements to inspire me, or gently washing my fingers in the basin outside with a bamboo ladle. It was all wonderful! Each movement is like a silent poem celebrating the present moment. The body becomes an instrument of harmony. Rather than colliding with things, it merges with them, honouring the objects, caressing the empty spaces and gracefully adorning the passage of time.

Turning everyday actions into rituals

Returning to France and the monastery, I took great care to be present in my movements. This is facilitated by the fact that we used lots of traditional greetings (bending the body forward with the hands pressed together), bowing and particular movements to enter or leave rooms . . . In regular society, it's different of course. So I would like to suggest a couple of little touches – simple movements to help you inhabit your body in harmony.

LEARNING TO SHUT DOORS

. . . and to open them, of course! The idea is to do all this is silence. No slamming, no noise: it's about closing doors with perfect technique, slowly and carefully, with controlled movements. What's more, by doing this, you'll be considerably reducing the everyday noise pollution in our towns and cities, thus doing a service to humanity into the bargain.

MINDFULNESS IN THE ART OF CHOPPING VEGETABLES

This can be done quickly. The idea is to feel your movements, in real time, when you're cooking. The kitchen is the perfect place because the flavours and smells, the spices and other aromatics all encourage us to savour the moment. Each movement is performed consciously, in the silence of the end of the day.

You'll find the process really relaxing, as you breathe in the aroma of the meal you're preparing, in an atmosphere of calm . . . or not! Because what I've just described is the perfect situation: no kids milling around under your feet, no head full of work stress, no partner complaining and plenty of time – glorious time – to prepare the meal . . . A dream scenario, isn't it?

In reality, daily life is often considerably less peaceful, I admit. But mindful movements as I have described do not require any particular environment. You can do this in the overcharged atmosphere of the end of the day, in a crowded restaurant or in the street. Even if it's just for a minute. Then take a break to wipe one of the kids' noses and start again. The most important thing with these two rituals is to practise them often. Very often. In brief snatches. This gets your mind used to a new way of being, so you lay the foundations for a spirituality of the everyday and the wisdom that goes with it.

PART THREE

―――――――

Practising silence

$$\left(6 \right)$$

A silent retreat at home (method)

What's the best way to disconnect for one or two days, at home or elsewhere? Why not try a silent retreat? The idea is quite easily workable and holds a few hidden treasures that can accelerate your development.

In the following pages, you'll find various ideas to help you in your retreat. They are simple suggestions, based on experience, to adapt to your situation. If you only have a few hours alone during the day, the previous day's preparations are also beneficial as a way of starting off in the best conditions.

In any event, whether your retreat lasts three hours or two days, entering the realm of Noble Silence, respectfully, through the Gateway of Concentration, can only be beneficial.

PREPARATION

Everything begins the day before, or a few days before. This is when you take the decision to enter into the experience, inwardly prepare yourself for the change of rhythm and gather a few tools or accessories to help you with your silent retreat.

Overcoming our guilt

A few years ago, I was lucky enough to visit a psychotherapist by the name of Madame Gabrielle Bastian, a woman of great wisdom. One day, when I was complaining once again about falling short of the accomplished and profound person I aspired to be, she replied with a knowing smile, 'But Kankyo, what you're describing there is someone in their seventies who has negotiated life's challenges over time and gathered their fruits. You're only 28 . . . Give yourself some time to learn!' Her words were like a therapeutic electric shock, and I immediately stopped chasing an unattainable ideal.

Or rather, I decided to move calmly towards it, making gradual progress. It's a bit like someone wanting to climb Mount Everest: if he finds himself from one day to the next at the foot of the majestic mountain wearing sandals, he's very likely to be in for a big shock and an immediate descent (unless our hero is discouraged in advance and decides to take the next plane home). If he takes the time to train, buy the right equipment and study the terrain, however, the moun-tain will open up to him bit by bit and the challenge will become achievable. In short, it's all a question of timing and . . . accepting your temporary limits.

So to embark on our retreat, we're going to begin by off-loading our guilt! By letting go of our guilt about being too stressed, not cool enough, a bad parent . . . the choice is yours. You'll start out as an 'imperfect' person and progress towards something else, which is normal. Sometimes, when

I'm giving a talk, during questions from the audience, someone will say, 'Oh no, meditation's not for me, I'm too hyper!' But that's precisely the point! Meditation isn't just for calm, controlled people; quite the contrary. Just like silence, it teaches us to sit down *with* our supposed imperfection, in order to fully accept it.

So you may very well begin your retreat feeling guilty about not doing enough for your children, your family, your job, your elderly parents or poverty in Africa. Or regretting that you're too sensitive, too lazy, not cool enough, that you lack confidence, or whatever. This feeling of guilt or inadequacy may be the emotion you will overcome during your silent retreat. It's possible (perhaps even likely) that it will disappear of its own accord, extinguished like a fire that has suddenly burnt up all its fuel.

Good nourishment

There's no point in hiding it, going from noise to calm is a real challenge. The change can be brutal, or even destabilising, and you will need some celestial – or entirely terrestrial – nourishment in the form of good food to help you.

REWARD YOURSELF WITH DELICIOUS FOOD

Unless you're combining silence with a fast (go crazy, why don't you!), you'll need several meals during your retreat. I cannot urge you enough to take great care over them and make them sources of pleasure. Seek out and line up some tasty, organic treats a few days before, appreciate the freshness of the ingredients and delight in their colours . . . You'll need a few carefully chosen foods, for their nutritional value of course, but above all for their flavour.

Staying silent and slowing down is a difficult undertaking, in which pleasure follows afterwards. Meals can be a reward, an interlude of pure pleasure between two periods of self-discipline. They let you harmoniously alternate between effort and satisfaction.

These tasty meals really are the symbol of a successful retreat. Because if the programme you've arranged is too arduous, discouragement could rear its head. The (unpronounceable) psychologist Mihaly Csikszentmihalyi captures this perfectly in his book *Flow – The Classic Work on How to Achieve Happiness*. Following a study conducted across several different cultures and generations, researchers have discovered the universal secret of happiness. I really recommend that you explore this fascinating book. In essence, the idea is to have objectives, desires and goals in our lives that give us pleasure but that also – and this is the magic prerequisite – require a little effort to achieve. The book describes a process that constantly oscillates between effort and pleasure, very much what this silent retreat entails. So your programme might include, for example, twenty minutes of silence without doing anything, getting bored if possible, followed by the rewards of a delicious meal.

INSPIRING BOOKS AS SPIRITUAL NOURISHMENT

Once again, the choice is yours: you could finally force yourself to read that enormous tome on 'new communication tools' (your boss will be pleased) or place a few inspiring books on your coffee table, choosing a wide and appealing selection.

After a few hours of silence, our mind becomes much more open to new ideas and new points of view. This is perhaps the time to give it fuel for thought with books on the meaning of life, understanding the human soul, a little bit of psychology or some travel writing. It's up to you . . .

For some suggestions, I've provided a little list of inspiring books (and videos) at the end of this book.

Set your limits and warn those around you

Some monasteries adopt the following procedure: anyone who wants to spend a few days immersed in Noble Silence attaches a label that reads 'Keeping Silent' to their clothes. That way, their colleagues scrupulously avoid talking to them during the allotted time. Why not use the same approach if you're with your family, for a few hours or a few days?

To go through with this change of behaviour with people around you, you'll need to be sure of your decision. Set your limits, explain and tell them about the benefits you expect for yourself and those close to you. You'll probably have to deal with some criticism or teasing. A piece of friendly advice: stay stoical and watch the storm pass by.

You can also keep in mind an important point that will help you remain calm in any situation: you don't need to convince anyone! Other people may not agree or understand. It doesn't matter. The main thing is to follow your own path, gently but surely.

Digital retreat and planned disappearance

We've now arrived at one of the crucial points in all of this: your digital retreat. To take full advantage of the silence, you'll have to turn off your usual communication devices: smartphone, computer, landline, tablet, etc.

CHANGING OUR RELATIONSHIP TO THE WORLD

Press the 'off' button, and you suddenly experience a completely different relationship to the world. For years, we've become accustomed to being permanently connected to each other via the internet. It's reassuring and often makes us feel less alone, as if we have a wide audience for our actions and are surrounded by a human community. I know certain people who make sense of their lives by posting their point of view to the world each day. So, far be it from me to dismiss these new technologies and the digital world lock, stock and barrel. However, on a silent retreat, the element of solitude is essential. It allows you to truly settle and learn a new way of being with yourself.

So for a successful retreat, you're going to need to disconnect completely. Turn off any phones and computers, and – after a little moment of panic – savour your rediscovered freedom!

How does it work? After announcing your retreat on Twitter (naturally!), place all your digital equipment as far out of sight as possible. Take a seat, breathe and open your eyes to take in your current surroundings. Or go over to the window to take a nice, peaceful look at what's happening outside. Disconnecting allows us to refocus on the present moment and the place where we are. Here, there, right away! This simple fact in itself is very relaxing.

The problem is that social media and communication apps ultimately create a sort of permanent tension. Presenting our lives on these different platforms has the side effect of preventing many of us from fully living the experience of the moment. As a result, many people are permanently running ahead of time: they are there with us, but at the same time, they are thinking about how to communicate the experience to the world (photo, text, tweet, etc.). A hyper-information society in which settling down, simply *being*, has lost its meaning.

By turning off all your digital devices, after a few moments of emptiness, a new relationship to the world appears, generating a profound sense of well-being. And all this begins the day before the retreat.

A planned disappearance

It's the day before the big day! There are various things that will make your disappearance from the virtual world (internet) go more smoothly:

- A message on your answerphone;
- Turning on your email's automatic holiday response;
- A phone call to your friends and family to reassure them.

The benefits of this are twofold. Not only do you free your mind to concentrate on other things, but you also commit yourself to staying silent. Having announced your plan to your entourage, it would be difficult to give up halfway without looking like a fraud . . . One of my friends gave up smoking that way. He went on and on about quitting so much that he would have lost any shred of credibility if he'd started again. By letting everyone know about your retreat and how long it lasts, you'll be held hostage to it, forcing you to stay the course and, above all . . . getting yourself some peace and quiet for a few days!

But better still: when people hear about your plan, it will arouse their curiosity and probably inspire some imitators. Others will be sure to ask how it went and about its effects, so you'll be able to help spread this beneficial spiritual practice: so once again, the benefits are twofold!

DURING THE RETREAT

Whether your retreat lasts two days, a day or a few hours, here's a selection of ideas to make the most of it. Naturally, you won't be able to do everything. Just pick out a few points. The risk of an exhaustive programme would be a retreat with the same intensity or stress levels as your everyday life.

And, ultimately, a programme won't necessarily be needed. It certainly provides a reassuring guide; but after a few similar experiences, at the end of your tenth retreat, for example, (yes, you do develop a taste for it!) you'll delight in planning nothing at all and just allowing yourself to live. But prior to attaining this enviable state of wisdom, here are a few pointers to help you take full advantage of these periods of silence in which time slows down, and – mindfully – savour a few fundamental experiences.

Getting bored or the art of looking out of the window

During a retreat in India, I found myself shut away for almost a week. As an entirely voluntary prisoner, in case you were worrying. It was part of a traditional ayurvedic purification ritual called *Shirodhara*, during which you receive intensive treatments with warm oil, all over the body and especially on the forehead, which involves the practitioner carefully sweeping a stream of healing oil across your forehead from right to left. The treatment lasts a few very long minutes, producing a sort of echo inside the body, an almost hypnotic oscillation. All of this is intended to bring about a sort of reboot of the cells. Aside from the fact that this age-old technique strangely reminded me of EMDR (Eye Movement Desensitisation and Reprocessing therapy), patients are regarded throughout the treatment as newborn babies. So they are firmly encouraged to remain in their rooms, not least to avoid any risk of infection.

This was the start of a whole new experience . . . Sitting in front of my window, I entertained myself by watching the cows, deer and birds pass by, lamenting their absence when they didn't show up. Most of the time, to be frank, there was nothing on the horizon, apart from a few motionless trees. Not even a nagging clock to mark out the passing time. Nothing. Nothing but an uncomfortable chair, a bed, an almost empty wardrobe and my niggling thoughts. I experienced lots of other things during that four-week trip. Unexpected encounters, fascinating Hindu rituals, memorable people and places. Lots of amazing things to fuel my story-telling on long winter evenings. But what I remember most of all are those unremarkable hours in front of my window. That was where I learnt the most. With nothing to do, no friends to talk to, I found myself for the first time in my life in the Great Void. At this point, many important things seem trivial and life itself takes on new contours. During that week, I went from annoyance to depression to joy, and finally to a profound calm. All thanks to a complete silence: of words, eyes, movements and . . . thoughts.

In your own home, you can begin with thirty minutes or

an hour in front of the window, with a stopwatch, so that you can really let go. And in a spirit of great friendship, I'd like to wish you a profoundly boring experience!

Eating your meals in silence

How wonderful it is to eat meals in silence. This is what we do every day at the monastery and I can really see the difference between these meals and lunches eaten hurriedly in the corner of a bar or on a railway platform. Because eating in silence makes several things possible.

First of all, and this is fundamental, it allows us to appreciate our good fortune, amongst our planet's seven billion human beings, in having something to eat. Before meals, numerous spiritual masters advise sparing a thought of gratitude for all the fortunate circumstances that have made this possible. Beyond any religious implication, it seems to me to be a very good way of honouring the meal we're about to eat. When my nephews were young, we always used to begin by putting our hands together and reciting this phrase: 'Thank you to everyone for having prepared this good meal'. As well as a subtle suggestion to my little guests that they didn't pull a face if the menu happened not to involve chips, the aim was to help them realise that none of the food arrived on the table by chance. We also sometimes ate our meals in silence, alternating with a few memorable mealtimes of riotous giggling (naturally, these were occasional meals, and the task is much harder for parents on a daily basis).

But that's not all. Eating in silence also – and most importantly – allows you to savour the dishes, explore their flavours and take the time to chew your food properly. To eat mindfully and to bring each mouthful to a close. It aids digestion and relaxes our breathing – and we can inwardly congratulate ourselves on our talents as a cook!

Finally, a meal eaten in calm helps the internal organs to function. If the stomach is relaxed, it will work all the better, and what could be more relaxing than the prospect of a little silence and time? It even seems, according to certain spiritual traditions, that at this point, when full consciousness appears, we absorb subtle, luminous energies with the power to strengthen our health and well-being.

Leaving the house . . . differently

Being a tourist in your own town often creates a feeling of strangeness, like an invitation to adopt a new perspective. I have regularly explored my city in new ways, looking up at the skies or cruising down the river. Because a silent retreat doesn't force you to become a recluse in your own home. Instead, it's about doing things differently, mindfully, at a slower pace.

In Chapter 3, I suggested a few exercises relating to the eyes, which are perfectly suitable for your retreat. In this way, two energies can coexist, inside and outside, in the home and outdoors, in an alternation that is quite close to ordinary life. However, as you might have suspected, the idea is not to spend your days outdoors, but to treat yourself to a few escapades and explorations of the world, whilst filled with your inner silence. Outside, make sure that you walk more slowly, stop often, look up at the trees or the pigeons . . . and savour the amazing pleasure of taking your time when everyone else is rushing around.

Take notes . . . for afterwards

During these few days or few hours, numerous ideas or impressions will pass through your mind. Realisations, questions, desires, ideas for improvements. It would be of great benefit to note some of these down. At the beginning, particularly if unpleasant emotions appear, take the time to write everything down wholesale, without worrying about style, just to get things down on paper and get rid of them. Give it a try: having a notebook within reach gives you a sort of outlet. Negative ideas are put down there, away from you, leaving your head much freer.

Later, the notebook can be used to take stock or to note down the new direction(s) you're planning for your life. Once again: when it's written down, it's documented and – logically – it's no longer an idea floating in the air . . . A first step towards your dreams and achieving them!

After your retreat, to rediscover the emotions, sensations and well-being you experienced, re-read your notes frequently. They will be like a positive anchor point during your everyday life. A resource. Your notebook will also be the symbol of everything you're capable of accomplishing in embracing your Life. Or like a point of departure, if you continue to fill the pages with your thoughts and developments.

And then . . .

Meditate, sing, dance, cook (see Chapter 5) or do anything else described in the previous chapters.

And enjoy your retreat!

Silence in our actions,
or ethical spirituality

THE EARTH: A VERY PATIENT MOTHER

Seen from the skies, planet Earth reveals an amazing variety of landscapes. Colours, reliefs, expanses of sea: all these splendours offer themselves up to anyone willing to see them! At daybreak or nightfall, beside the ocean or at the summit of a hill, a mystery is present... It is up to us to tiptoe towards it and make a connection.

I recently heard an interview with the Native American activist and actor Russell Means, who spoke with sadness of his people's difficulty in practising their spirituality linked to nature (to the Earth) in our society dominated by materialism.

The interview has now resurfaced at a time when American Indians, or Native Americans, are still fighting in the north of the US to preserve their lands from exploitation for oil. For me, this message is essential. It says it all. What could be more important than getting up each day to watch the sun rise and plant our feet in the Earth?

Unfortunately, some of our fellow humans seem to have other priorities: buying stuff, tarmacking the fields, building factories, domesticating nature . . . When I hear Native Americans, I feel less alone but, like them, I'm saddened by the way our societies have evolved up to now. Sad but optimistic, as the trend does seem to be changing. Numerous initiatives are flourishing around the world with the aim of preserving, caring, simplifying, slowing down, etc.

Often, I imagine the Earth as a mother, lovingly observing the frenetic activities of her children in the four corners of the globe. They rush, fight, dig, catch fish, bury their rubbish, etc. They're so badly behaved she doesn't know where to start! When the mess gets too bad, she snaps her fingers and we experience some freak weather or a natural disaster: mother brings the schoolyard back into line before letting her children go out to play again. Looking at the things we do around the world, I see us human beings as unruly children, gradually learning from our mistakes. And most importantly, each time one of us falls, he or she can explain to the others how to stay on their feet. Some listen, others don't, the explanation will need repeating, calmly and at length. The route is a long one and the Earth is very patient.

But here's an idea: what if we entered the age of reason? If we left the schoolyard to go to college? If you join the tribe, we'll have lots of fun, you'll see. We'll explore new places, invent a new world, and better still . . . mother will be pleased!

A RETURN TO SIMPLICITY

All things being equal, you'll have made a lot of progress since the beginning of this book (otherwise, hop to it! Down to work!). A case in point is the issue we talked about at length in Chapter 1, in the section on 'Emptiness'. The feeling of emptiness inside that, when it appears, impels us to go out in order to forget the distress it causes, orders us to turn on the TV, or commands us to fill the gap with some compulsive shopping. Sometimes, these purchases appear reasonable, but if you really think about it, was that new smartphone actually necessary?

By overcoming this emptiness inside us, or learning to do so gradually, we will also free ourselves from this irrepressible need to fill it. And free the Earth from an incalculable quantity of rubbish in the making. It's as simple as that. Master Wang-Genh (the abbot of the Ryumonji monastery) recently had this to say on the subject: 'When human beings sit down in meditation, they become angels. And the good they do for the Earth is amazing . . .' You couldn't put it better. This was the spirit in which we marked the COP 21 conference with '24 hours of meditation for the Earth'.

But the path of meditation is not the only way to regain our freedom. Sometimes, simply realising the amount of time we spend shopping, the energy it takes to keep up with fashion or the carbon footprint of a certain vegetable flown in from the other side of the world is enough to quash our desire to consume. Personally, as the emptiness inside me subsided, I was able to establish a few simple principles to guide my relationship to consumption. I wanted to share them with you here, as a sort of exchange. They're simply examples, without wanting to pin any guilt on anyone or set rules for everyone. It's up to each individual to see how they could apply to his or her life, in the short, medium or long term.

Ethical shopping

A few years ago, I read this quote from the Vietnamese Zen master Thich Nhat Hanh: 'If you consume objects created through suffering, you sow the seeds of suffering within yourself.' The pertinence of this teaching was brought home to me even more sharply by the building that collapsed in Bangladesh in 2013. Nearly 1,200 people died, most of them women who worked in unsafe conditions to make our clothes. The Rana Plaza disaster: lives sacrificed for our beauty on the other side of the world. A truly sad aspect of the principle of interdependence.

Since then, I have meticulously checked the provenance of the products I buy. How can I enjoy a particular (famous) chocolate bar that relies on child labour in Africa? I won't mention any brands, but if the subject interests you, do some research on the internet; you'll find that many companies are implicated.

I now also always do my homework on how and where my clothes were made. I'm haunted by the image of a young girl bent over her sewing machine, her back bent from days of intense labour. She didn't choose to be there, and her life is contained within the walls of the factory. This is what's known as modern slavery. Luckily, there is something we can do. By exerting pressure, for example, on the brands in question, threatening them with a boycott, in order to bring about change. The shareholders will do without 0.000001% of their dividends, and my girl will have the time to go and enjoy the sunlight with her boyfriend.

Of course, we could also wait for the world to change by itself or for the very rich to agree to become a little less rich (or for water to stop getting us wet). But it sometimes seems to me that encouraging a new awareness, through a boycott or a petition, in a spirit of gentleness and calm, is of benefit to everyone. It's up to you . . .

Happy sobriety, a tribute to Pierre Rabhi

I might as well admit that ethical shopping has made life more complicated. At first, I looked for alternative products: fair trade clothes, French-made goods, etc. It was a laborious process, because labels only tell part of the story. Sometimes, they try to mislead you by only stating the last link in the manufacturing chain (see the wonderful work carried out by organisations like the Clean Clothes Campaign). So another solution emerged of its own accord: inaction! Or rather what the environmentalist and campaigner Pierre Rabhi calls 'happy austerity'*. I buy a lot, lot less . . . And congratulate myself every day on all these revolutionary non-purchases!

But Rome wasn't built in a day. And the path of what I call 'voluptuous abstinence' took several years to embrace. At the beginning, like many people, I was a frenetic consumer. Back when I was a student (studying law), I was lucky enough to receive a grant and also to work as a babysitter. At the slightest attack of the blues – which were very frequent back then – I roamed the city centre, buying clothes, good things to eat, books, CDs or anything else to give myself a little treat. The result was temporary relief, generally followed by a new feeling of emptiness, particularly in the wallet! At that point, I was unaware that this emptiness inside is a bottomless chasm, and that only a paradigm shift, a reconciliation, can bring peace.

Today, having been observed and accepted, my emotions are much less intense. I very rarely go into shops and don't think about shopping or imagine myself owning a particular object. And I much prefer spending time in the forest or with friends than in a shopping centre.

But there's more! The concept of 'happy sobriety' is so fashionable in France, and other places, because it offers sustainable happiness to those who embrace it. More than that: it even offers a sort of jubilation, the tenacious pleasure that I call voluptuous abstinence. Not consuming is pleasurable, does you good, makes you smile and conceals a whole host of hidden benefits. For example:

....

* Pierre Rabhi, *Vers la sobriété heureuse*, 2010.

- Having more time to do other things: see friends, read a book, do karaoke, sing in the rain, watch a river flow by, etc;
- Saving money so you can afford really worthwhile things: a course on non-violent communication, support for humanitarian projects, building up a nest egg to give you a sense of security . . . or whatever is important to you (yes, I admit we're talking about consumption here too, but on a different level);
- Joining the tribe of 'benevolent revolutionaries'! Not buying is a political act: you rediscover the feeling of being able to influence the world, taking control of your life, and deciding to contribute to a better future. And once again, it does you good!

VEGETARIANISM OR THE ART
OF NOT EATING YOUR FRIENDS

The ethical treatment of animals is probably one of the areas in which we are making the fastest progress, and rightly so. This has been helped by terrifying reports on the everyday reality of abattoirs (for both people and animals), as well as our shared desire to protect the Earth from overconsumption. This is one of my favourite subjects. Yet although it's something close to my heart, writing this section is a real challenge. The emotional impact of animal suffering is so great that I find myself distraught, caught between anger (a very poor advisor) and despair (which is no help at all). Faced with the torture we inflict on animals, I'm like a child discovering the existence of the atom bomb, asking over and over again: but why? Writing with delicacy and compassion is a real struggle, so I'll try to tackle the subject by connecting with the beauty present in each living being . . .

The other evening, I was invited to dinner in the home of a couple who have practised Buddhism for nearly thirty years. They're charming people, highly educated members of well-to-do Parisian society. During the aperitif, commenting on the fact that I'm a vegan, the husband exclaimed with a tear in his eye: 'Oh, I completely understand, animal suffering is something I just can't stand!' And then they served up caramelised pork that had been cooking all afternoon . . .

'Non-human' animals

To get a better understanding of the subject, let's spend a few moments thinking about Western history . . . For many centuries, it seemed necessary for humans to affirm their superiority over the other species. The different theologies played a significant part in this by placing mankind at the centre of creation. God had created man in His image, giving him a superior role and special qualities. Fine. But in exchange, God had also given us a number of quite feminine duties, such as taking care of our fellow creatures, watching over them and maintaining harmony. The conquest of new territories, however, soon led to a feeling of vulnerability, and we needed to affirm our power in order to reassure ourselves. So taking a very narrow view of the sacred texts, we granted ourselves the right of life and death over creation. And we all know the consequences.

But now, in line with the natural evolution of human beings, a completely new perspective is required.

And this begins with the terminology itself. The way we name things says a lot about our relationship to them. In light of recent discoveries about the species, increasing numbers of researchers and academics are distinguishing between 'human animals' and 'non-human animals'. The overall category being 'animals'. Spending hours in forests and meadows, in the company of horses, cats, birds and various insects, I'm delighted by this new classification! And there are benefits for people, or rather human animals, in exchange. Just think: as animals, our sensory abilities (hearing, sight, touch, etc.) deserve recognition or even celebration. As animals, we can gradually discover the wonderful blessing of inhabiting our bodies rather than our heads. As animals, we can embrace the spontaneity and immediacy of the moment, instinctively protected by a new and powerful community ethic.

But then a crucial question arises: what is the justification for eating our fellow animals? Or this one: do our five minutes of pleasure when eating a steak justify the terrible suffering that preceded them?

The wisdom of American Indians . . . or the Buddha

It's not just how we relate to other animals; this idea encompasses all growing, living things. Once again, we must look to Native Americans, to those who live close to nature, in order learn how to relate to the Earth. Before chopping down a tree, they take the time to gather the tribe for a final ceremony. They thank the sentient being that is about to give its life, tell it what will become of it through their songs, and celebrate its existence and the benefits it bestowed. This gratitude demonstrates a high form of awareness, a high degree of evolution and applied knowledge of the principle of interdependence that governs the operation of the world.

On the other side of the world, in India, the stories of the Buddha's former lives also offer us a few gems. These stories are called the Jatakas: sort of metaphorical tales in which the everyday sits alongside the miraculous. In one of his lives, it's said that the Buddha offered his thigh to a mother tiger who was close to death, so that she could regain her strength to feed her cubs. A far cry from the North American tiger-hunters posing on Facebook with their trophies and big guns . . .

Abstention, a non-violent choice

So vegetarianism, or even veganism, appears to be the path of non-violence, or *Ahimsa*, the principle embraced by Gandhi. Declining consumption and trade that are rooted in violence brings numerous benefits. Silence in our actions has unexpected virtues that can deliver or strengthen our daily well-being.

FOR THE GOOD OF OUR CELLS

After a long process of waiting, endless transport, pain, cold, thirst, abuse, etc., our little cow Daisy emerges from the abattoir as a deboned carcass, chopped into pieces. Each of these pieces that lands on our plate (or not) is impregnated with a substantial layer of suffering. Scientific tests have shown that secretions of stress and other hormones peak at the point of slaughter. So the meat we are sold, whether it comes from mammals or fish, is filled with stress and tainted with various hormones. By eating it, we are also ingesting these things. Is it any wonder that we can feel heavy, ill at ease or even distressed after a meal?

In contrast, if you opt for vegetable proteins, pulses or tofu, and find pleasure in exploring new tastes and new recipes, your cells feel light! An abundance of vegetables produces colourful, appetising plates of food, with no risk to your health, in fact quite the opposite. I have been a vegetarian for dozens of years and a vegan for the past three, and suffer from no deficiencies, with the exception of the well publicised lack of vitamin D that I share with three quarters of my fellow Alsace inhabitants in winter. And if I sometimes suffer from a slightly acid stomach, this is mainly due to my coffee addiction (I admit it!).

BEING AT PEACE AND FEELING CONNECTED: A WELCOME SIDE EFFECT

Since I made the decision to become a vegan, I have felt at peace, with the sensation of doing what needs to be done. Of course, I've had to give up on the classic cheese raclette with potatoes that I would tuck into each winter, but the sacrifice is small compared to all the sensations of well-being that regularly flow through me. The emotion of happiness at living a life completely in harmony with your values.

I very often address this issue of values with people who come for hypnotherapy sessions. To change our lives, our behaviour or even our habits, we should be clear about what is most important for us: everything that life would be a failure without. For some, this might be feeling free or safe, helping others, travelling, starting a family, being the best in their sport, etc. When you achieve these things or your life is moving in the right direction, inner silence appears, naturally, like a welcome side effect or a bonus gift.

Personally, being in harmony with nature is one of my most important values. A successful day, for example, is one in which I've been able to hear the birdsong and watch the sun rise (I did this in Paris recently and it was magical!). And I can't imagine getting up in the morning with the seeds of animal suffering inside me. When I go into the neighbouring meadow to say hello to my four-legged Icelandic friends, they gather confidently around me, snorting happily. Maybe they can sense that I've lost the predatory aspect found in carnivores. Of course, I have no scientific studies to corroborate these ideas, just the firmly held belief that this lifestyle entails a profound change to my internal programming. Less aggression, stress, tension . . . and much more inner relaxation, laughter, hedonism and contemplation of the world's beauty!

$$\begin{array}{c}\boxed{8}\end{array}$$

Some exercises for every day

As you know, I believe that if you want to change your inner workings, regular practice is required. Exercises need to be done each day, like little daily rituals (remember the fundamental rule of the 3 'R's and 4 'S's!).

So here are some exercises in silence to accompany you in your new life. It is a good idea to note down what you feel and discover each time . . . and to re-read these notes before doing the exercise the next time (that way, not only will you make progress, but you will also feel more motivated).

....

EXERCISE 1: TAKING VISUAL PAUSES

In front of your computer, focus on a point, an icon or an area of the screen. Channel your gaze in a specific direction. Then allow a new perception of your body to appear. A new perception of the world

....

around you . . . And breathe! Three-minute visual pauses every 2 hours.

EXERCISE 2: REGULARLY RELAXING YOUR JAW

Install a 'gong' or 'mindfulness bell' app on your phone. Numerous apps have been developed and allow you to set your own frequency, for example every hour. When the gong sounds, relax your jaw and feel the effect on your body's relaxation as a whole (see page 108, 'Pulling a dopey face'). Two minutes every hour.

EXERCISE 3: YOUR FIRST WAKING THOUGHT

Each morning, take notice of your first thought, as soon as you wake up, even before getting out of bed. Let it pass by and observe the next one . . . and begin the day mindfully, having regained control of the machine. To be done each morning. (For some detailed explanations of this fundamental exercise, see my TEDx talk from January 2016: 'Eyes wide open in the present moment' – subtitled in English.)

EXERCISE 4: SILENT LUNCHES

Once or twice a week, make a deliberate choice to eat your lunch alone and in silence. Freely chosen, luminous silence. A lunchbreak during which you really take the time to chew each mouthful and to savour your meal. You'll discover that time stands still and a vast expanse of tranquillity can emerge, in the middle of a working day.

Further exploration:
Resources and little bits of magic

CHAPTER 1 –
THE VIRTUE OF SILENCE

On the idea of accepting yourself as you are and recon-
ciling yourself with your imperfections, see Pema
Chödrön's book *When Things Fall Apart: Heart Advice
for Difficult Times*.

To observe the splendour of a simple and profound life:
look for videos featuring Sri Ma Anandamayi.

For a better understanding of the way our minds work and
the different types of thoughts, watch my TEDx talk
(with English subtitles): 'Eyes wide open in the present
moment', Kankyo Tannier, 2016.

CHAPTER 2 –
SILENT INSPIRATION

On the subject of animals

Laila del Monte's work on intuitive communication with
animals: www.lailadelmonte.com.

The highly original thinking of an English scientist: Rupert

Sheldrake and morphic fields in *The Rebirth of Nature* (Bantam, 1991).

A book of animal behaviour for a better understanding of cats: Desmond Morris, *Catwatching* (Jonathan Cape, 1986).

For a spiritual retreat

Now that meditation has become fashionable, there is an extremely wide choice. However, I would advise you to choose your destination carefully. Buddhist monasteries generously open their doors to lay people and followers of other religions. If rituals take place, you can simply take them as an experience of the present moment and harmony. To help you find a place for your retreat with experienced teachers, these are some English language websites:

IN EUROPE:

www.zen-azi.org: includes the Zen monastery of La Gendronnière, an incredible place in France, near Blois, in the middle of an immense forest. Numerous retreats for beginners, teaching translated into English.

www.meditation-zen.org: the monastery where I lived for over fifteen years and where I still spend a lot of time, run by Master Olivier Reigen Wang-Genh – teaching translated into English.

www.izauk.org: provides a list of Zen Buddhist groups/
dojos in the UK.

IN THE US, CANADA, NEW ZEALAND
AND AUSTRALIA:

Numerous organisations and temples, with certified
teachers, are listed on the website of the Sõtõ Zen
School: www.global.sotozen-net.or.jp

CHAPTER 3 –
VISUAL SILENCE

To calm your eyes: a white wall and a few minutes at your
disposal in which to do nothing.
On the abbess Shundo Aoyama, a venerable 85-year-old
nun and a marvellous example of a spiritual life: the
book *Zen Seeds*.

CHAPTER 4 –
VERBAL SILENCE

The Hidden Dimension by Edward T. Hall.
The Doors of Perception by Aldous Huxley.
For a retreat in complete silence: see the retreats run by
the Vipassana Association, which carries on the work
of Master S.N. Goenka, or the dates for silent retreats
(held 3 times per year) on www.meditation-zen.org
(monastery in France).

CHAPTER 5 –
BODILY SILENCE

On the influence of the body on the mind: watch the video of Amy Cuddy's TED talk ('Your body language shapes who you are') on www.ted.org. This very entertaining and dynamic talk has been translated into numerous languages.

For the Feldenkrais method, which invites us to discover and inhabit our bodies through micro-movements: see www.feldenkrais.co.uk.

To find out about the Urasenke tea ceremony: numerous videos are available on the net. My advice is to watch them with the sound turned off.

CHAPTER 6 –
A SILENT RETREAT AT HOME (METHOD)

Flow by Mihali Csikszentmihalyi.

An ayurvedic retreat in India: the Panchakarma process is discussed in the following article: www.dailyzen.fr/ayurveda-india.

Contemplation: the work of my talented photographer friend Manuela Böhme on: mboheme.tumblr.com.

CHAPTER 7 –
SILENCE IN OUR ACTIONS,
OR ETHICAL SPIRITUALITY

Corine Pelluchon's essential book *Le Manifeste animaliste* (English translation underway).

The activities of the animal rights organisation PETA.

A Plea for the Animals by the Buddhist master Mathieu Ricard, who treats his subject with great compassion and without apportioning blame: a model of wisdom!

The Man Who Planted Trees by Jean Giono, (Peter Owen, 1989).

yellow kite

books to help you live a good life

Join the conversation and tell
us how you live a #goodlife

🐦 @yellowkitebooks
f YellowKiteBooks
P Yellow Kite Books
📷 YellowKiteBooks